W9-BZU-159

"Most of us with college degrees forget what it was like to graduate, but not Erica Reitz. Filled with good sense on a wide variety of topics that matter, *After College* provides a one-stop resource for young adults who want to honor Christ at a time in life when everything is changing. Both graduates and those who care to help graduates will benefit from Reitz's counsel."

Peter Krol, president, DiscipleMakers campus ministry

"Big changes and transitions often force people to ask big questions: Who am I? Why am I here? What am I doing? *After College* provides a helpful guide to wrestle with those questions in a way that is inspiring and hopeful. Erica is a keen listener: she listens well to God, recent research and student stories to offer a roadmap for success in today's world."

Derek Melleby, executive director, OneLife Institute, author of *Make College Count*

"It's far too common! College students graduate and then crash into analysis paralysis, getting stuck on questions like: 'Where do I go?' 'What should I do?' 'How will I get to where I want (or God wants me) to go?' We've needed a reasoned and compelling answer to the post-college crisis for decades, and Reitz has delivered brilliantly in *After College*. Every college graduate needs this book in hand, preferably six months before graduation. Every disciple-making ministry leader should know its content inside and out."

Brian N. Frye, national collegiate strategist, North American Mission Board

"Reitz has written an intensely practical book that tackles every possible challenge a newly graduating student might face. This is done in a way that empowers young adults in making choices that will help them thrive, not just survive, as they emerge into adulthood. Throughout the book Reitz interlaces scriptural stories about moments of transition that both encourage and instruct. Because I care about preparing my students to launch into their next phase of faithful living as followers of Christ, *After College* is destined to become required reading in my capstone course."

Jana Sundene, associate professor of Christian ministries, Trinity International University, coauthor of *Shaping the Journey of Emerging Adults*

"This is a must-read for graduating seniors and an excellent resource for everyone seeking to live intentionally. Covering the full spectrum of life's most basic issues, *After College* offers an insightful, practical, and biblical guide to fortify and encourage faithful transition. Erica Young Reitz manages to convey useful advice with an inspirational voice."

Paul J. McNulty, president, Grove City College

"*After College* provides a thoughtful, biblically sound, pragmatic, and much-needed resource for college seniors and recent graduates. Erica Reitz addresses well the issues of isolation, disillusionment, and frustration while also providing hope and a vision of flourishing for this generation. This book connects young adults with honest expectations for the real world. As someone who has seen many students struggle to faithfully find their way after graduation, I could not imagine a more important topic to address. Erica responsibly tackles this subject with passion and a heart for helping young adults follow Jesus with every aspect of their lives."

Vince Burens, president and CEO, CCO

"*After College* offers evangelical Christians profound insights about grappling with postcollegiate life in today's swiftly changing world. Beautifully written by Erica Young Reitz, it seamlessly interweaves real-life stories from recent college graduates with astute quotations from famous writers, biblical paradigms with sociological studies, and practical how-to advice with inspirational hopefulness. At once both personal and professional, Reitz shares the triumphs and trials of her own experience in order to help readers discern God's calling in both church and society."

Crystal L. Downing, author of *Changing Signs of Truth* and *Salvation from Cinema*

"From the opening chapter, 'Go to an Unknown Land,' Erica Young Reitz invites emerging adults on a virtual tour of life in the land beyond college. She conducts the tour from a deeply personal perspective, fully engaging the passions, possibilities, dreams, and dangers travelers will experience on their journey. Reitz's greatest gift lies in her choice to refrain from telling the reader what to do and instead make room for showing the way to enter the unknown land 'with a known God (who knows you).'"

Richard R. Dunn, lead pastor, Fellowship Evangelical Free Church, Knoxville, author of *Shaping the Spiritual Life of Students*

AFTER COLLEGE

NAVIGATING TRANSITIONS,

RELATIONSHIPS AND FAITH

ERICA YOUNG REITZ

IVP Books

An imprint of InterVarsity Press
Downers Grove, Illinois

InterVarsity Press
P.O. Box 1400, Downers Grove, IL 60515-1426
ivpress.com
email@ivpress.com

©2016 by Erica Young Reitz

All rights reserved. No part of this book may be reproduced in any form without written permission from InterVarsity Press.

InterVarsity Press® is the book-publishing division of InterVarsity Christian Fellowship/USA®, a movement of students and faculty active on campus at hundreds of universities, colleges and schools of nursing in the United States of America, and a member movement of the International Fellowship of Evangelical Students. For information about local and regional activities, visit intervarsity.org.

All Scripture quotations, unless otherwise indicated, are taken from THE HOLY BIBLE, NEW INTERNATIONAL VERSION®, NIV® Copyright © 1973, 1978, 1984, 2011 by Biblica, Inc.™ Used by permission. All rights reserved worldwide.

While any stories in this book are true, some names and identifying information may have been changed to protect the privacy of individuals.

Lyrics from "Painting Pictures of Egypt": © 1999 Sara Groves Music (admin. by Music Services). All Rights Reserved. ASCAP. Used by permission.

Cover design: Cindy Kiple
Interior design: Daniel van Loon
Images: model car on map: Imagesource/Glow Images
        map and key: DNY59/iStockphoto

ISBN 978-0-8308-4460-9 (print)
ISBN 978-0-8308-9436-9 (digital)

Printed in the United States of America ∞

 As a member of the Green Press Initiative, InterVarsity Press is committed to protecting the environment and to the responsible use of natural resources. To learn more, visit greenpressinitiative.org.

Library of Congress Cataloging-in-Publication Data

Names: Reitz, Erica Young, 1980- author.
Title: After college : navigating transitions, relationships, and faith /
  Erica Young Reitz.
Description: Downers Grove : InterVarsity Press, 2016. | Includes
  bibliographical references.
Identifiers: LCCN 2016010694 (print) | LCCN 2016011633 (ebook) | ISBN
  9780830844609 (pbk. : alk. paper) | ISBN 9780830894369 (eBook)
Subjects: LCSH: Young adults—Religious life. | Christian life.
Classification: LCC BV4529.2 .R45 2016 (print) | LCC BV4529.2 (ebook) | DDC
  248.8/34—dc23
LC record available at http://lccn.loc.gov/2016010694

P 21 20 19 18 17 16 15 14 13 12 11 10 9 8 7 6

Y 34 33 32 31 30 29 28 27 26 25 24 23 22 21 20 19

For our Senior EXIT students past, present and future,
and for every recent college graduate,
igbok (it's gonna be okay)

CONTENTS

AUTHOR'S NOTE

YOU ARE ABOUT TO ENCOUNTER the struggle and success stories of many alumni. While all quotes and stories are real, some names and identifying details have been changed to protect the privacy of individuals.

As you enter this book and join your story with theirs, I invite you to find one or more friends to read it with you. My hope is that any individual will find encouragement in these pages, but I believe the experience will be richer and more meaningful if shared with others.

Enjoy the journey!

Note on terminology: When referring to individuals, I've opted to use the casual "alum" instead of the formal "alumna" or "alumnus."

WHY THIS BOOK?

So, are you ready for life after college?

Leaving the gates of university life often comes with the expectation that we're ready for what's on the other side. But what does readiness even mean? Some students feel ready in September of their senior year (get me out of here!) while others—who may actually be more equipped for the "real world" than they realize—dread college coming to a close. In the scurry of résumé preparations and job applications, it's easy to reduce readiness to our emotions about entering adulthood or to a list of key items necessary for life on our own.

But preparedness is not just about securing a job and apartment, or a paycheck in hand. It's about much more.

It's about preparing not just for a career but for a life of faithfulness in a complex world. It's about connecting what's happened in the classroom for the last four years to our calling—to what we will do and who we will be after college. It's about practical tools and resources for navigating the transition in areas such as budgeting, finding community and making decisions. It's about having a healthy perspective and proper expectations. It's about finding answers to questions we may not even know we should be asking. And it's about knowing it's going to be okay when we don't have the answers right away.

Working with hundreds of seniors and recent graduates over the last decade, I have learned that leaving college does not automatically mean readiness for what comes next. As evidenced by the growing conversation in higher education regarding senior-year preparedness, lots of recent graduates are floundering on many fronts as they emerge into adulthood. Observing this trend forced my colleagues and me to ask, "What can we do during the college years, especially senior year, to prepare our students for life after graduation?"

Our answer led to the launch of a senior-year experience called Senior EXIT. With a team of colaborers, I have spent the last ten years helping seniors at Penn State University prepare for the transition into the next phase. Through Senior EXIT we address both the philosophical and the practical realities of post-college life. We help seniors "pack their bags" with the resources they will need to faithfully navigate the changes, challenges and choices of the first year out. Our hope is not only to prepare students to successfully exit college but also to see them flourish in the months and *years* that follow.

This book is a culmination of my master's studies and professional experience working with seniors and recent graduates, but it is also personal. My own transition out of college wasn't the smoothest. Though I had a good head on my shoulders, a great educational experience, strong faith and a loving family, entering the "real world" after seventeen straight years of school (grade school, middle school, high school and college) came as a shock to the system in ways no one had prepared me to consider. I struggled with loneliness as my close friends and I scattered across the country, I felt directionless in my career, and I didn't know how to manage my minimal income. On a deeper level, I wrestled with questions of faith, doubt and identity. I was used to playing the role of a student, and I didn't know how to measure success in a system that wasn't set up like college. Simply put, I struggled to make life work in many areas, and—for a time—I thought I was the only one who felt this way.

I'm certain my own story shapes my passion for working with college seniors. I love being able to address topics that are crucial for a successful transition from a faith-based perspective. As one graduating senior put it, "College [professors, advisers, etc.] stresses the importance of preparing for graduation and the job, but they cover none of the topics that concern me most." The transition is multi-faceted, and anyone going through it needs support on *all* fronts. This is where this book steps in.

This book is about pursing faithfulness in life after college. It can feel overwhelming as we consider all the ways we're called to be faithful as well as all the potential challenges. Don't worry; we'll take this step by step, topic by topic. Though the issues related to the transition are interwoven, we'll take this on in three parts. We'll start by looking at what it means to be faithful in our relationship with Christ—how to cultivate real faith in the face of real-world demands. Then we'll discuss faithfulness to community—how to find and foster healthy relationships with others. Last we'll talk about faithfulness to our calling—how to discern our vocation and honor God in our output to the world.

You will find that this book primarily addresses those who identify as Christ-followers and who desire to follow him in every area of life. That said, I invite any student or recent graduate to glean from these topics, regardless of what you currently believe about Jesus or Christianity. Whether you have been following Jesus most of your life, you just met him in college or you are not sure about him, I welcome you to enter in and transition well.

PART ONE

REAL FAITH

FAITHFUL TO CHRIST

ONE

"GO TO AN UNKNOWN LAND"

TRUSTING A FAMILIAR GOD
FOR UNFAMILIAR TIMES

I dwell in possibility.

EMILY DICKINSON

IN THE COLD NOVEMBER of her first year out of college, Natalia sat by the fireplace in her parents' home, weeping. Bone-tired, overworked and lonely, she thought, *This is not what life is supposed to be like.* She was working seventy to eighty hours a week just to stay afloat in a demanding marketing job, she had no time to make new friends and she longed to be in a dating relationship—something she assumed would have happened in college. Her stomach hurt every Sunday evening when she thought about facing another week with her impossible boss, catty coworkers and overflowing inbox. Stuck on a treadmill, Natalia felt desperate for just one of the luxuries she had enjoyed while she was a student: an hour to sit in a coffee shop with a friend or to play the piano alone. She said leaving college felt like the "world had been ripped out from under me." Nothing felt settled or familiar. Natalia confessed, "I felt inadequate and incapable of making life work." Desperate for something familiar, Natalia made frequent trips to her parents' home on the weekends. She longed for something known in the midst of so much upheaval and uncertainty.

As we step into the great unknown of life after college, it's important to know we are not alone. We journey forward in the footsteps of a long line of leavers—an ancient history of God's people who have abandoned all that is familiar to follow a call into uncharted territory.

Consider Abraham—a man called by God to leave his country, his people and his father's household in Harran for a new dream.[1] At the ripe age of seventy-five, he hears God say, "Go." Give up everything.

The LORD had said to Abram, "Go from your country, your people and your father's household to the land I will show you.

"I will make you into a great nation,
    and I will bless you;
I will make your name great,
    and you will be a blessing.
I will bless those who bless you,
    and whoever curses you I will curse;
and all peoples on earth
    will be blessed through you." (Genesis 12:1-3)

When we understand the cultural context, this ask is *huge*. God calls Abraham to abandon all he has ever known and everyone who knows him. He must say goodbye forever to his kinship group—his entire network of relationships and social support.[2] There's no technology that will connect him to his people or hometown ever again. Instead, if he says yes to God he will be separated from all he's ever known by approximately five hundred miles—that's a one *month* journey by caravan (at a twenty-mile-per-day clip).[3] He will never again walk the dusty paths his feet have travelled every day, smell the salty air after a hard rain, see his aging father's smile or hear the roar of laughter as he and his friends throw their heads back in the glow of a night fire. It is goodbye for good.

As the male heir, Abraham is slated to inherit everything from his father, securing his place in society and in the family line.[4] This too he must give up in order to follow God. Will he choose to forsake everything in order to heed God's call? Will he cut ties with the land, his family, his inheritance and his people—a bond built over seven decades? Leave his whole life behind to embrace God's promise?

The Scripture says, "Abram went" (Genesis 12:4). He decides to trust God—to take him at his word. Abraham has faith that God will provide anew everything that he has asked Abraham to give up.[5] As we step into life after college, we too are called to forsake the familiar to embrace something new. As exciting as this time may be, it's also marked by great uncertainty.[6] We trade a familiar place and our familiar purpose within it for a new reality. Leaving college may mean we have to let go of certain ways of doing things, embrace new roles, redefine relationships and say goodbye to people we care about. As we enter the unknown, we can look to Abraham and be encouraged by his faith in an uncertain time as well as by God's faithfulness to him.

We can also take comfort from Abraham's example when our expectations don't match our reality. Abraham steps out in faith only to find his path littered with trial. He encounters plagues, persecution, detours and doubts long before reaching the fulfillment of God's plan. At one point he has to reroute to Egypt because the very land God has told him he'll possess is brittle with drought. Not to mention that the wife who is supposed to bear him a child is still barren at age sixty-five. The fruition of God's plan is not looking so good.

The oppression and struggles cause Abraham to disbelieve God and question his character. Can God really be trusted to deliver on his word? Abraham wonders, "O Sovereign LORD, how can I be sure that I will actually possess [the land you promised]?" (Genesis 15:8 NLT). Perhaps you too may question whether the God you followed during college can be trusted in this time of transition. Maybe you find yourself throwing your hands up, wondering, *How can I be sure you really have a plan, God?* In Abraham's fears and frustration, God is gracious and patient. He reminds him of his character and promise:

> Do not be afraid, Abram.
>> I am your shield,
>> your very great reward. . . .
>
> *I am the* LORD, who brought you out of Ur of the Chaldeans to give you this land to take possession of it. (Genesis 15:1, 7)

The same God who led him in Ur is also the God of Abraham's transition. Likewise, the God of your college years—the God of Abraham—is the same God who leads you in the joy and challenge of the transition into the next phase. He doesn't change his tune when our circumstances change. His character and promises are constant, even in dynamic times. Everything may be shifting around you, but God, our rock, remains the sure and solid place we find our footing. He is the God who pursues, promises and provides—even after college.

PREPARING TO ENTER THE UNKNOWN

Looking to God and his character is a crucial part of preparing for any transitional time. So are the practices and perspective we choose in the everyday. Though there are many things we cannot predict as we enter the unknown, we can manage our expectations, choose intentional actions and adopt healthy heart attitudes.

Before we address these, it's important to realize that our day-to-day actions, attitudes and expectations are always connected to a bigger picture: our core beliefs, our worldview. Whether we're aware of it or not, we all believe in something, value something, worship something. Every day we direct our affection and desires toward something, and often we do it without even knowing it.[7] We may be chasing money, power, influence, comfort, pleasure, fame, good looks or smarts. Why? Because of our deepest beliefs. We may claim we love God or have a Christian worldview, but we must examine our lives to see what our behaviors say about what we really believe.

If we don't know what we believe or if our claims don't carry into our everyday actions, then we'll likely adopt the worldview of those around us or fill in the blanks with something insufficient. If we're going to thrive beyond college, we need a robust worldview that makes sense of our deepest pain, greatest dreams and everything in between.[8] It is our Christian worldview—shaped by the biblical story of creation, fall, redemption and restoration—that fully prepares us to expect difficult life experiences without losing hope in the midst of them.

Not sure what you believe or what it means to have a Christian worldview? Check out Christian Worldview: A Student's Guide *by Philip Graham Ryken.*

Accurate expectations. "The first year out was one of the hardest years of my life," reports Curt. He moved to inner-city Baltimore for a job with Teach for America, a position that stretched him in ways his college classes and student teaching stint did not. Curt also left campus at the height of his social game with a strong support network. President of his Christian fellowship group, he had countless friends, an active community life and college ministers who invested in him. Then he moved to a city where he knew no one. In addition to the adjustment to an unknown place, he faced significant challenges in his family life that year. Everything seemed to hit him at once.

Another alum, Kate, describes her first year this way: "It's much rougher than I thought. . . . I thought things would just play out, and they didn't. I don't have friends, I don't have a job and I hang out with my parents every night!" Upon graduation Kate could not find a job, so she chose to move back home with her parents. She struggled to find friends with similar values, to connect to a vibrant church, to make ends meet financially and to keep proper perspective.

My own experiences as a graduate validate what Curt and Kate say about their first few months out of school. I moved to a small town called State College in what felt like the middle of nowhere, Pennsylvania. Though referred to by locals as the "Happy Valley," it felt more valley than happy. I struggled to find my place and purpose in a new location; there were dismal days that made me feel anxious, lonely and depressed (the often gray sky didn't help). On my worst days I used to get up and go through the motions of a morning routine only to find myself paralyzed by feelings of despair. *Is this what life after college is like? Did I make a mistake in moving here?*

I share these stories because they represent a narrative I encounter again and again: life after college comes with challenges. If your transition is easier than you expected, give thanks. But if it's not, you're not alone! Sometimes it's hard because we're not prepared, but it's also hard because we're going through a major transition.

Perhaps you cannot imagine any hitches in your first strides out of school. For many alumni that initial stretch offers a welcome change to the confines of college. Making money, living on your own, doing work in a field you love—it feels like the best of times. But even so, you will inevitably hit a bump in the road—a heartbreak, rejection from a job or promotion you want, financial struggle, relational conflict. Life after college is a sweet time, but not necessarily because it lacks obstacles. Thriving in the next phase is not so much about avoiding challenges as about learning how to navigate them. And it's about managing our expectations within them.

Though many recent graduates feel unprepared, there are also those who enter the transition with a robust worldview and realistic expectations. They prepare for potential obstacles and gain tools necessary for navigating change. They still find that life after college is hard at times. But also very good!

Jackie shares that her transition went more smoothly than she envisioned. She credits her success to her own preparedness as well as her patience with the transition. Without skyscraper expectations for everything to go perfectly, Jackie was able to keep sane and let things unfold in time. Instead of stressing because the field that she'd trained for (occupational therapy) was not what she wanted to do, she chose to trust God, take her time with the questions that surfaced and invite others to help her discern her career path. This process led to a job-shadowing opportunity with a physician assistant. After that, Jackie landed a nursing assistant job that would expose her to a variety of areas within the field and allow her to further clarify her vocation. In Jackie's words, "It's a confusing time, but the biggest thing that kept me calm was realizing I don't have to be rushed as I figure things out."

When we keep a level head and manage our expectations, we position ourselves for a more successful transition. If we assume we may hit a bump, rather than being surprised when we do, we will likely move over it with hope and grace instead of allowing our disappointment to send us into a downward spiral.

Intentional actions. One of the biggest challenges of Christian life is aligning our beliefs with our behaviors. Many of us flounder because we're not sure how to manage unmet expectations or we choose actions (or inactions) that send us down unhealthy paths.[9] We may wake up one day to realize *I don't even know how I got here.* Countless little decisions (or indecisions) add up to a life we never meant to live.

Stephanie admits, "I crashed and burned right after college." She struggled to set boundaries in a social service job with endless client needs; she wasn't sure how to be an effective employee and she didn't know how to ask for help. When she found a church, she failed to plug in beyond Sunday morning. Because there were few people in a similar life stage and the church was a forty-five-minute drive away, it felt like too much effort to do more, especially in the midst of her exhausting schedule. Stephanie reflects, "So much is handed to you when you're in college. If you want to be a Christian, you simply show up to a certain hall at certain time. After college, you have to go after everything, and I didn't know how."

A challenging first year led to an even worse second. To supplement her income, Stephanie started bartending a block away from home and moved in with a friend from work—someone who was not a healthy influence. Working at the bar made it easy to start drinking—at first to relieve stress, then as a lifestyle. The bar became Stephanie's primary place of connection. She says, "When I realized I wasn't making friends and connecting in an adult way, I was desperate and lonely." Patterns from her past resurfaced as she slipped into drinking and hooking up. After two years of burnout and bad choices, Stephanie realized, "I was soulless and dead inside. . . . This was not the life I intended to live."

Because she started with a college education and a job offer, Stephanie thought she should "have it all together"—as if having her ducks in a row marked the arrival into adulthood. But there were so many things she wasn't prepared for, and she didn't know where to turn. In her words, "I failed because I had this misconception that I should have my life in order, love my job, and have a great community. But when I didn't have it all figured out, I didn't know where to ask for help . . . or even that I could."

Trying to prove to others that we've "arrived" is not the goal. These years are about making choices that will help us successfully *emerge into* adulthood. The risk of floundering is real. We can guard against it by preparing for challenges, asking for help and choosing intentional actions. Though the landscape is thick with temptations, a life of flourishing in the next phase is possible. There are many struggle stories, but also many success stories!

Robert, a graduate who successfully transitioned into a new job and location, was both intentional about preparing and thoughtful about his choices. He moved two hundred miles from his entire support network and his fiancée just after getting engaged. Before making the move he researched churches in the area and asked for recommendations. During his first week of work (and still without furniture in his apartment) he took the initiative to check out a small group nearby. While not the right fit, it was a start. Despite out-of-town weekend commitments over the following weeks, Robert settled on a church within the first month. He got plugged in to a small group, which became the start of a new friendship network. Among other healthy decisions, he chose to live on a monthly budget that included giving as well as long-term priorities, including paying off student debt. He also managed his time and finances with his future wife in mind. They approached decisions as a team even though they would not be married or living together for another year.

Though this transitional time was not without challenges, Robert had the perspective and tools to navigate them. He says,

> I would not say that my first year after graduation was easy. The tension of being distant from valued relationships has never really gone away. I didn't always know exactly what to do in every circumstance, but I had tools in my toolbox that helped me deal with expected challenges. This gave me peace and confidence in those areas and gave me more time and energy to deal with the unanticipated challenges that always come up.

Robert took intentional action because he was equipped, but also because he desired to align his beliefs with his behaviors. We can make wise choices when we're prepared with practical life skills—not just in terms of *what* to do, but also in the whys and hows. When we know deep down *why* something (like finding a church or managing money) matters (belief) as well as *how* we actually put one foot in front of the other to go after it (behavior), we can pursue faithfulness.

Healthy heart attitudes. As we start that first job, move into a new neighborhood or begin a grad school program, we will inevitably meet people who do not share our vision and values. Our world is filled with competing worldviews and value systems (nihilism, atheism, individualism, consumerism and so on) that we'll encounter every day. As our beliefs bump up against others', we may find it hard to share hope while still holding on to our own. We may be tempted toward attitudes of selfishness, cynicism or despair.

In a baccalaureate address to a group of Stanford graduates, Jim Wallis, CEO of Sojourners, stated, "The big struggle of our times . . . is the fundamental choice between cynicism and hope. . . . Hope is not a feeling; it is a decision."[10] Though there are many things we cannot control about transitional times, we can choose our attitude. On most days we will have a decision to make about the perspective we adopt: cynicism or hope? Apathy or anticipation? Fear or trust?

We can enter the postgraduate years with a mindset that will wreck us or we can adopt the opposite. We can choose to believe that a life of flourishing is possible, even if the first few months or years out are bumpy. *Despite* our circumstances, hope believes that the story is not over—good can and will prevail. Stronger than mere optimism, hope allows us to recognize that things are not at their best while trusting in a greater reality—that God is at work, reconciling *all* things to himself, making *all* things right. Someday life on earth will be like it is in heaven. *That's* perspective!

One of the most encouraging things I can share about all of these alumni stories and my own is that we each (eventually) turned to Jesus and chose hope in a time of transition. Or, perhaps better put, Jesus chose and chased after us, and we surrendered to his love. Though we had moments of despair and days of doubt, we continued to cling to the character and promises of God. Beyond just believing *in* God, we decided to believe God—that he is who he says he is and his promises are true.[11] There were definitely days I disbelieved and many mornings when I prayed that God would give me the faith to even have faith. There were days of desperation, frustration and heartache, but never a day without a decision to make: cynicism or hope? Apathy or anticipation? Fear or trust?

Robert, who desired to choose hope, shares a bit about how his worldview affected his attitude after college:

> There is one obstacle that I do not recall needing to deal with very much: fear. I understood the gravity of what I was taking on all at once, and truthfully I did feel overwhelmed at times. But I also felt prepared and capable of dealing with it. I had doubts that making so many big transitions was the right decision. But because I know that God is sovereign over every square inch of my life, I had peace that he had prepared the way for me.

My hope is that you take some time to prepare for the road ahead. I also hope that you "dwell in possibility." This Emily Dickinson line is hope in phrase form—a great mantra for life after college. This attitude welcomes and expects good things. It anticipates that something wonderful is around that next corner. If we experience confusion, exhaustion or frustration for a time, it indicates that we are on the brink of discovery. In fact, perhaps the more frustrated we are the closer we are to that revelation. When we dwell in possibility, the world is a fascinating place where we get to participate in the work of a God who delights to unfurl his goodness before our eyes. He longs to lead us into a life of flourishing.

ENTER THE UNKNOWN WITH
A KNOWN GOD (WHO KNOWS YOU)

Just as Abraham stepped out in faith, not knowing where he was going except that he was to leave Harran, we too must trust God to reveal his plan and purpose. As you go, God will "show you" (Genesis 12:1).

But it's not the kind of revelation where you get the entire roadmap up front. The Hebrew word for "show" in this verse literally means "*as you are going*, I will show you.*" Borrowing from Doctorow, Anne Lamott says that life is like driving a car at night: you can only see as far as your headlights. She says, "You don't have to see where you are going, you don't have to see your destination or everything you will pass along the way. You just have to see two or three feet ahead of you."[12] If we saw our whole life plan mapped out before us, we'd anticipate all the hard parts—the steep climbs and dark valleys—and we'd likely try to run or find an alternate route, missing exactly what God plans or allows for our good and his glory. We may not have a blueprint, but we do have a guide who will light each step of our way (Psalm 119:105).

Surely we will encounter bumps in the road. Maybe we already have. In vulnerable moments, our reaction and actions often reveal the bare bones of our belief. In my conversations with alumni a consistent theme stands out: unknown times and postcollege trials become the proving ground for faith, forcing us to wrestle through until we hopefully emerge with deeper belief than before. When trials come, our loss, pain or uncertainty may bring us to a crossroads. Will we believe that God knows us—that he sees exactly what we are going through and holds us close? Or will we sink into the sea of our own struggle, disbelieving his presence and sovereignty in our lives?

In my first year out of college, I experienced the most significant loss up to that point in my life: I had my heart broken. It may sound trivial now, but at the time it was so painful I wanted to throw up every day for weeks. This postcollege trial became a defining faith moment as I had to choose between shaking my fist at God or clinging to Christ for dear life. Feeling hurt and broken, I told a close friend from college that I was ready to say "screw it" when it came to seeking God's best, especially for my dating life. I felt like God had screwed me over, so why not do the same to him? "Besides," I rationalized, "if I get hurt again, at least it will be on my terms." As I confided in my friend she reminded me that we had a belief system that offered a greater hope and higher standard. Her faith sustained my own, pushing me in the path of God rather than self.

As I look back on that time, I see a tender, caring God who knows me. He knew I needed that friend at that moment to steer me toward Jesus. He also provided a friend in my new community who was going through nearly the exact same thing. God spoke to me in ways I could connect to, such as through the Psalms or the Rilke poem "Autumn," which arrived in a random book from my father the week I was hurting the most. God poured out so much good in the months and years that followed. Not to mention all of the good that came from removing that relationship at that time. A gaping space opened in my life, and though I was tempted to fill it in unhealthy ways, God gave me himself. He also gave me friends and mentors who helped me through deep inner healing. I met with our prayer team at church, and I experienced God more intimately than ever before. God knows us. He knows what we need better than we do. And he is a known God—a God whose tried and true character can be trusted for good in our lives.

As God continues to fulfill the promise he made to Abraham, it leads to generations of God's people trusting him and recalling his character. For example, the book of Joshua recounts the faith of the Israelites as God parts the Jordan River during flood season for them to cross. While God holds back the waters, he commands Joshua to enlist his leaders to build a memorial. Each leader must remove a stone from the middle of the dry ground and carry it to the other side. There they build a monument that will forever mark the moment of God's miracle and provision (Joshua 4:1-7). God invites us to recall his faithfulness—to remember that his hand carries us, especially in the middle of our own raging rivers. Each time we recall God's faithfulness in a former situation, we stack a metaphorical rock, creating a monument on which to fix our eyes in times of distress and doubt. As we remember his goodness, God re-members us, putting our fragmented, broken selves back together.[13]

Not only is God's goodness the same yesterday, today and forever, but also he is the one who promises to bless us, keep us and fulfill his good purposes through us. The same man, Abraham, who was called to an unknown place received a promise that carried through generations. A promise that is as true today as it was centuries ago: God is building his kingdom through broken people, blessing those who choose him and making them great in him. This promise radically changed Abraham. It will change us too if we choose to cling to a familiar, *good* God in these unfamiliar times.

GOING DEEPER

1. What are your greatest hopes and concerns right now?

2. In what ways are you entering or already in the unknown? What feels most uncertain or unfamiliar? Why?

3. What comfort or lesson can you take from Abraham's story?

4. Preparing for a life of faithfulness involves accurate expectations, intentional actions and healthy heart attitudes. What is one thing you can do to better prepare?

5. Can you recall a time when God demonstrated his faithfulness to you? What metaphorical rocks can you stack as a reminder of God's character?

6. What broken or hurting part of your life do you need God to remember? How can you invite him or others in?

Scripture study: Genesis 12–25, especially 12:1-4; 15:1, 7-8; Joshua 4:1-9

Recommended reading:
Byron Borger, ed., *Serious Dreams: Bold Ideas for the Rest of Your Life* (Square Halo Books, 2015).

Steven Garber, *The Fabric of Faithfulness: Weaving Together Belief and Behavior*, expanded ed. (Downers Grove, IL: InterVarsity Press, 2007).

Meg Jay, *The Defining Decade: Why Your Twenties Matter—and How to Make the Most of Them Now* (New York: Twelve/Hachette Book Group, 2012).

TWO

IN TRANSITION

EMBRACING CHANGE

I've been painting pictures of Egypt,

Leaving out what it lacks

The future feels so hard

And I wanna go back!

But the places that used to fit me

Cannot hold the things I've learned

Those roads were closed off to me

While my back was turned!

SARA GROVES, "PAINTING PICTURES OF EGYPT"

ABOUT NINE MONTHS after graduation, Faye questioned, "Is it normal that I want to pack my bags and ask my parents to pick me up and take me home?" After ongoing struggles with a corrupt landlord, a financial setback due to a cycling accident and the loneliness that came from grieving the loss of her former community from college, Faye felt like giving up. She had graduated with a similar idealism to her peers who wanted to change the world, and Faye thought she could handle the setbacks that would come. She believed her faith was strong enough in the face of struggle, but she reached a breaking point. She had seen such sinful parts of humanity (and herself) that it forced her to think, *I'm losing the fight.* Despite the things that were going well (she loved her job and she found a healthy church), Faye was exhausted. She just wanted to go home.

Being in transition is hard! Simply trying to make it in the world while we're going through one of the most difficult in-between times can cause any of us to want to phone a parent or friend for a life-flight rescue out of it. While parts of the transition may be going well, other parts may not be unfolding as we had hoped. The transition out of college is complex and multifaceted, which makes it hard to prepare for. Some seniors feel prepared when they have a job offer and know where they're headed after graduation. Others may have these in order but do not feel emotionally ready to leave their friends or financially prepared to handle loan payments. Regardless of our perceived readiness, we all enter a transitional time when we graduate. As you prepare to enter the unknown, or as you are currently there, it's helpful to know what to expect when going through a transitional time and why transitions matter.

IN TRANSITION

From life's small to big changes, everyone processes transitions differently. Research into stages of transition has helped me and others name what's happening, both internally and externally, and navigate the process. Transition theorist William Bridges talks about the difference between transitions and change, suggesting that *change* is what's happening on the outside (with our situation and external circumstances) whereas *transition* is what's happening on the inside (with us personally and internally). The effect of the transition and the change that triggered it are not directly proportional.[1] When it comes to graduating from college, the change (college is over) may impact you very differently than it does your peers. Be prepared for you and your friends to experience different emotions and challenges within the same change. Allow yourself to transition as you need to—without comparing yourself to someone else's process. There may be parts of the change you take in stride that others find overwhelming, and vice versa. Be faithful to respond to what God may be teaching *you* in the process.

Though our personality and previous experience uniquely shape the way we undergo transitions, there are certain aspects of transitions that are generalizable. When it comes to major life changes, there are those who will try to fast forward the process and those who will seek to avoid it altogether. Though our bent will likely be toward one of these, neither are healthy approaches to being in transition.

It's important to make the most of the transition—to milk it for all its worth.[2] Transitions are some of the most life-changing, shaping times we encounter, and we don't want to miss out, rush through or run away. We must acknowledge that "transitions take time, often from three months to three years."[3] Though it's crucial to connect our transition to a desired end or hopeful outcome (a picture or vision of ourselves fully transitioned), we need to allow ourselves to be in transition before we reach that end.[4]

CYCLES OF TRANSITION

As you enter the transition, it will be helpful to keep in mind that transitions are made up of cycles. Though different theorists may describe the cycle differently, transitions contain a necessary ending, a middle time and a new beginning. Bridges's cycle includes the following:

- ending
- neutral zone
- new beginning[5]

Endings: finishing well. Each time we go through a transition, we need to accept that an ending is happening, and we need to allow ourselves to fully process the ending in order to finish well. Often we don't talk about endings because we like to move on to the next thing. We live in a progress-driven society; dwelling on an ending counters our cultural values. Endings can trigger emotions of fear or grief, so it's easy to ignore the fact that an ending needs to happen (or is happening) because we simply don't want to face it.

I spent the summer before my senior year in Chifeng, China, teaching English to Chinese high school students. As we prepared for our final week there, our team leader encouraged us with 2 Corinthians 8:10-11: "And here is my judgment about what is best for you in this matter. Last year you were the first not only to give but also to have the desire to do so. *Now finish the work*, so that your eager willingness to do it may be matched by your completion of it, according to your means." Though these verses are an appeal to God's people in Corinth to continue giving financially to the poor, Paul's point (as was my team leader's) is this: finish strong. Oftentimes it's much easier to start something than to bring it to full completion. The excitement of stepping off the plane in Beijing at the beginning of our trip seemed like a distant memory in those final weeks when we were depleted and homesick but unsure how to say goodbye to the people we had come to love. It would have been tempting to bypass the ending—to slack off in the last week, pack our bags early and avoid saying goodbye to the students we taught because it's easier than finishing strong.

Instead, we took our team leader's charge. We said yes to every invitation to eat in the homes of our students (knowing it would only make it more painful to part), we stayed up late practicing for a performance we'd been asked to give at the final banquet, we dealt with interpersonal conflict on our team, we prayed hard, laughed hard and worked hard. And in our final hour, through the glass panes of a train about to leave Chifeng we looked back with tear-filled eyes at wide smiles, waving hands and full hearts. We finished strong.

When it comes to endings, we need to finish well—as Jesus did (John 17:4). *What does it mean to finish well? How can you fully embrace the ending as you leave college?* It may mean finishing well in your classes, co- and extracurriculars, and relationships with peers, professors and roommates. For example:

- Have you given over to "senioritis" or are you completing your coursework, giving it your best even at the end?

- Do you have a role or responsibility on a sports team, within a club or in a fellowship group? Is there a younger leader you need to train before you leave?

- Is there a broken relationship you need to make right?

These are just a few of the many questions we could consider when it comes to ending well. There are students who finish strong, and there are students who avoid the necessary ending of leaving college. I know a student who graduated, left in a fury and failed to mend the broken relationships she had with two of her roommates. "College is over, so I don't see the point"—her attitude is the opposite of finishing well. On the flipside, I know students who stay engaged in their studies through finals week, sacrifice time to serve their campus fellowship groups even at the semester's end, initiate final meetings with their professors and mentors to thank them, and invest in friendships until the last hours.

During her senior year second semester I discipled Christine, who confessed she had "checked out" at the start of the year. Each time we met, she admitted that she struggled with staying present instead of looking ahead to the next thing (namely, her wedding, set for a month after graduation). As we discussed some of the heart attitudes that contributed to her senioritis, I asked, "What does it mean to be faithful this semester to the roles you currently play?" As we looked at her relationships and roles as a fiancée, student, daughter, sister, friend, roommate and leader, she made an action plan for faithfulness in each area. From her desire to have a sleepover with her sister before her wedding to her commitment to stop by the office of her adviser, she came up with concrete steps for finishing strong. In our final meeting together she reflected on the lessons God had been showing her over the past year. Her biggest takeaway: "Learning to be present."

Whether you are still in college or have already graduated, it's important to be present and embrace the ending component of the transition. Regardless of your undergraduate experience or emotions, college is ending or has come to an end. Any time something ends, we experience loss. It's important to name the loss and give ourselves space to grieve it. We may need to cry with close friends or take a long walk across campus alone. We may want to hole up in the library stacks or listen to loud music. We should also be prepared for the reality that the grieving process will continue beyond graduation. One alum, Andre, shares, "I was struck by the emptiness I felt when all of my friends were gone. I didn't realize how much I'd have to grieve that loss." As we do whatever it takes to embrace the end and grieve the change, let's also make sure we grieve with hope (1 Thessalonians 4:13). Life after college is *good*.

What else can we do to end well? A part of ending well involves a process of "dismantling"—metaphorically and literally. Picture a home remodel.[6] If we planned to renovate a bathroom and found water-logged drywall behind the tub tiles, we would remove it first. In the same way that it's crucial to take down the old sheetrock before hanging the new, ending college requires us to dismantle certain things before setting up the new thing (life after college). For example, we may need to dismantle the ways in which we are used to structuring our time or our approach and expectations when it comes to hanging out with friends, especially if they are no longer living close

by. Perhaps we will need to let go of our financial dependence on our
parents before we can begin life on our own.

There are countless ways in which we could go about the dismantling and ending process; however, the most important thing is that
we show up to it, ask God how we can be faithful in it and choose to
actually go through it. Let's finish strong.

Neutral zones: the in-between time. After we allow ourselves to
cycle through the ending, we will enter the neutral zone—an in-
between or fallow time. The neutral zone may be the hardest part of
the transition and the easiest to ignore. We may long for the past or
desire to rush to the future, so we fail to fully embrace the *in-between*
time. We can't just move from ending to new beginning like a quick
walk from west to east campus. We need to give ourselves time and
space to be in the middle.

In this in-between time we may experience distress—an emotion
that initially tells us something is wrong.[7] In the neutral zone many
recent alumni question, "Did I make a mistake in moving here?
Should I have taken a different job? Is this the wrong plan for me?" In
her first year out of college, Amy accepted a long-term subbing position for a former "Teacher of the Year." Fumbling to fill such huge
shoes, Amy was ready to quit by January. She spent most weekends
poring over lesson plans and crying. The methodology she'd been
trained in wasn't working, emails from frustrated parents filled her
inbox and every day brought a new question: What's a 403b? Where
can I find a field trip request form? How many assessments do I need
to accurately grade a child? She felt lost and overwhelmed. Leaving
seemed like the logical solution.

Just because something feels disorienting or distressing, it doesn't
mean we need to go somewhere else. We must watch out for the voices
that say there's an easier, sexier, less mundane path that we should be
on. Also, it's important to resist the temptation to assume that we
need to find something outside of ourselves or our situation to resolve

what we're experiencing at the moment.[8] There's a good chance we are exactly where we need to be; we just need to allow ourselves to be open to all God wants to show us in the in-between time. In retrospect Amy is so glad she did not leave. The stress of being in transition made the job feel impossible, but after the first-year fog lifted it became easier. Not only did it build skills and experience, but it also leap-frogged Amy into a successful teaching career.

Our minds are not always clear when we are in transition. In the Old Testament we read the story of God's people, the Israelites, whom a man named Moses leads through a time of significant transition: from captivity in Egypt to freedom in the Promised Land. During their in-between or literal wilderness time, the Israelites freak out and want to go back to Egypt. They remember days when they could eat fish, melons and cucumbers instead of desert manna (bland unleavened bread; Numbers 11:4-6). With irrational minds, they think they would be happier returning to back-breaking slave work than being in an in-between time! (Exodus 14:12). Though I'd never compare college to bonded slavery, there are parallels in the longing to go backward, especially in an in-between time. It's perfectly normal to miss college— to long for parts of the experience that we used to have. However, even in these emotions it's important to not dwell on the past to the point of failing to be in the present.

The neutral zone is strange. In its strangeness and unfamiliarity we may be tempted to rush our transition, cut it short or bypass it altogether. Similar to our cultural inability to do endings well, we are also not very good at waiting, middle times. We don't know how to allow ourselves to *be* in empty, fallow spaces. I'll never forget one of my Chinese students commenting on life in the United States: "Americans seem so anxious to fill the hour." How true. We are masterful at filling our time, at being busy, often in an effort to avoid being still or alone. We don't know how to face our inner self. Just wait in line at a grocery store or public restroom for a moment. It takes *seconds* before people start pulling out their phones, checking texts, updates and emails. We are anxious to fill the hour, the minute, the second. We don't know how to do otherwise.

In an experiment that explored our "capacity for solitude," people were asked to sit in silence for six to fifteen minutes without a book or device. "Many student subjects opted to give themselves mild electric shocks rather than sit alone with their thoughts."[9]

If we are going to allow ourselves to transition through the neutral zone, we need to make space to reflect and process. Reflection is not just a word for mystics and poets—it's essential for life as a disciple of Jesus. We need time to let our inner self relocate and reorient itself.[10] The same way a tree drops its leaves and enters a fallow time before making way for spring, we need to give ourselves over to this in-between rest time. Fully embracing it will allow us to prepare for what is new and next. We don't need to feel guilty or defensive about this time. We can choose it as a necessary part of the transition cycle.

We also need to be mindful that while wilderness times can bring some of the most significant spiritual growth, they can also bring great temptation. Because we're stressed, unsettled or lonely we may be tempted by old sin patterns or new struggles. We may be tempted to wander away, give up or give in. We may turn to an unhealthy relationship or start having one too many drinks at happy hour. We may pursue unhealthy outlets to deal with stress (for example, overworking, disordered eating, looking at pornography). When there's little accountability, as is often the case when we're trying to establish ourselves in a new community, we may start to forgo daily practices that keep us close to Jesus and far from sin.

How can we flee temptation? Let's look to the example of Jesus himself when he went through his own literal desert time before launching his public ministry (Luke 4:1-13). While in the wilderness, Jesus prays, fasts and rebukes Satan with the Word of God. We too can guard against temptation by choosing spiritual disciplines including praying, fasting and reading Scripture. Jesus was filled with the Holy Spirit, the same power we can rely on to resist sin and grow closer to God. In addition to clinging to Jesus and his example, it's important to find at least one other trusted friend or mentor to support us through the in-between time.

What else can we do to be faithful in the neutral zone? It can be as simple (and as difficult) as making time to read, pray, reflect and be still. It may mean a conscious effort to slow down, to stop *doing* and start *being* for a time. It may mean we take a hike outdoors or get off the Internet. Or it may mean we start a journal to log thoughts, ideas and questions that arise in this time. Consider, how can we create space to be honest with ourselves and God? If something "new" is not happening yet (job offer, grad school acceptance, meeting friends, finding a church), we can choose to accept that we're in an in-between time—it's normal; the new thing will come.

Instead of bypassing it, Kevin decided to deal with the in-between time head-on. For him that meant looking back on the past experience of college while also allowing himself to get excited about the future. The summer after graduation he took time to jot down memories, write poetry and keep a record of things he was thankful for. He also listened to songs that were important to him during college. Kevin says,

> I ended up being really melancholic in that summer. Maybe I hammed it up a bit because I'm more like that in general, but I wasn't opposed to having emotions. . . . I was enjoying the past with the perspective that I would be making a transition and leaving things behind. I wasn't comparing my future with my past, but I was willing to be open to a new experience.

Though there were points when the fallow time felt like grieving a death of people and the college town he'd come to love, Kevin realized that these friends and places were still there—they were just not in his life the same way. He also learned to rely on God, his constant during a changing time. In his daily devotions Kevin thanked God for his past and asked God to prepare him for the future. When he was tempted to believe that college was the best years of his life, God reminded him, "If life has been good, that's the best evidence that it will be good." It was reminders like these, which came through Kevin's daily practice of reading and praying, that kept him grounded in the middle time.

We often want to be where we are not (whether that's back at college or fully on to the next thing), but we were made for the everyday and mundane just as much as for life's mountaintop experiences. Think again of those Israelites in the desert. Not only do they forget all that God has done for them prior to their wilderness wandering, they also fail to give thanks for his provision in the everyday—sending fresh manna *every* morning and taking such tender care that after forty years of trekking through the desert their clothes and shoes do not wear out! (Deuteronomy 29:5).

In transitional times, it's easy to despise the manna—the provision of now as we long for what was or what could be. But let me encourage you that God is providing exactly what you need this day, and going back may not be as grand as you think (remember how stressed you were about that exam, or that person you crushed on, or that project deadline?). Each season of our lives has sweet times and challenges. Let's accurately remember the past, be fully present in the now and have faith for the future. *Give us today our daily bread.* Let us accept each provision as it comes, trusting in Jesus—our true Manna—who sustains and carries us. Take and eat.

New beginnings: the land God is bringing us to is good. As you persevere in the in-between time, trust that you will not be there forever—

it will break way to a new beginning. *How do we know when the ending is complete and we've been in the neutral zone long enough?* New beginnings aren't necessarily marked with a definitive start, like the dropping of the New Year's ball in Times Square.[11] Think back to other beginnings in your life (such as moving to a new place, beginning your first job, starting college): likely the start of the new thing was not perfect. New beginnings aren't clean cut, nor are they mechanical, like turning on a car or computer. We should expect a little mess and nuance. As poet Mary Oliver reminds us, "Most things that are important . . . lack a certain neatness."[12]

For some alumni, the new beginning may be that move to a new location or the start of that first job or graduate program. However, we need to keep the goal in mind—the goal is to *transition*, not just change locations or start something. Sometimes external change allows us to avoid the internal transition process that must take place. Entering the new beginning may not primarily entail a move or the start of a job but rather a new way of doing something—a new way of relating to the world.

If we have been faithful to the steps of the cycle that precede the new beginning, and if we have truly given ourselves the space to end well and reflect, we will likely gain a sense of the new beginning before it even happens. Perhaps God has even revealed a hope or promise to you in advance, as he often does with his people:

> See, the former things have taken place,
>   and new things I declare;
> before they spring into being
>   I announce them to you. (Isaiah 42:9)

We may have thoughts, dreams or desires during the in-between time that hint at the new beginning.[13] Perhaps we imagine what we want God to do in us, through us or around us. Maybe we envision ourselves doing something that we want to try. Or there is some learning from our classroom experience that we're excited to apply in a new job. As some of these hopes arise and are realized, it may mean the new beginning is taking shape. In the same way a hotel key card is pre-coded to open a door, as we become ready or "keyed-up" to welcome a new beginning, we will more easily find the opportunity we're looking for. It will click, opening us up to the new thing.[14]

Faye was nine months into a new job and location, and things were still not clicking. Though desperate for a way out, Faye knew she needed to stay. About three months later the new beginning began to take shape. Some of the tangible aspects of being in transition started to settle—for starters, she was no longer living on her friend's couch while her landlord refused to fix her apartment's frozen pipes. She was also starting to establish a sense of home in her location. She had friends to hang out with on the weekends, she could check out a library book and read it all day, and her newer coworkers started looking to her for answers (instead of her asking all the questions). Faye reflects, "That's when I felt like I'd finally transitioned."

Be patient with the process, especially if it feels like things aren't clicking right away or if you have no clue what might be next. Be kind to yourself and patient with God in the process. He is *always* doing a new thing. In fact, for the believer each day is a new beginning, with new mercies every morning (Lamentations 3:22-24). This should bring us great hope and strength to wait on God. We may be waiting for a certain kind of new beginning (such as that job offer) when the new thing God is doing is that of making us new in the attitude of our minds (Ephesians 4:23). We have the promises of new life and newness more abounding than anyone.

As you go through the process of leaving college and transitioning to postcollege life, keep in mind that though this transition is arguably one of the most difficult you will make up to this point, life is full of transitions. You will inevitably encounter other major and minor life changes in the months and years to come—even in the days to come.

We continually go through endings, neutral times and new beginnings, every day. Transitions are a normal and natural part of life, so let's surrender to the process, trusting that God has amazing things in store within *all* of it.

TIPS FOR THE TRANSITION

Each section above contains practices that we can embrace during transitional times. Here is a short summary of what has been discussed—a reminder list to help with our perspective and process:

- Don't rush or try to skip any parts of the transition.
- Leave well; finish strong.
- Grieve well (with hope); mourn the ending.
- Give yourself permission to be in the fallow place, the in-between time.
- Reflect and process. Schedule time *alone* to do this on a regular basis.
- Be attentive. Be mindful of internal things that may need to come to the surface.
- Be patient and gentle with yourself.
- Recall God's character; remember his goodness.

GOING DEEPER

1. Think back to a prior transition (such as the transition *into* college, the death of a family member, a major move or your parents' divorce). What lessons did you learn about yourself, life or God through that time? How might those insights apply to the transition out of college?

2. How do you think your personality style or past experience shapes the way you transition?

3. How do you approach endings? In-between times? New beginnings? Which part of the cycle is most challenging for you? Which
   do you think you do best and why?

4. Which part of the cycle do you think you are in right now? How
   can you be most faithful to being fully present in it?

5. What is one thing you will continue doing, start doing or stop doing
   when it comes to your attitude or actions in transitional times?

6. How can you invite others into your transition? What do you need
   prayer for most in this time?

Scripture study: Lamentations 3:22-24; Isaiah 42:9; John 17:4; 2 Corinthians 8:10-11; Ephesians 4:23; 1 Thessalonians 4:13

Recommended reading:

William Bridges, *Transitions: Making Sense of Life's Changes* (Cambridge,
   MA: Da Capo, 2004).

Chuck DeGroat, *Leaving Egypt: Finding God in the Wilderness Places*
   (Grand Rapids: Square Inch, 2011).

Jeff Manion, *The Land in Between: Finding God in Difficult Transitions*
   (Grand Rapids: Zondervan, 2013).

THREE

TAKE UP YOUR CROSS

FACING ADVERSITY

Faith is the gaze of the soul upon a saving God.

A. W. TOZER

"I OFTEN REFER TO MY first year out of college as 'the year from hell,'" says Curt. His two-year commitment to Teach for America brought him to a failing school in Baltimore, where he knew no one. He left his family and friends behind to start what became an impossible job; it took everything in him to try to control his chaotic classroom of fifth graders, and many days he did not succeed. Beyond the daily struggle to get up and teach another day, Curt faced adversity on a number of other fronts: he struggled to find friends, the woman he'd been "pseudo-seeing" broke off communication, his grandfather passed away and his dad was diagnosed with throat cancer. This was not what Curt pictured for his first year out of college.

In college Curt had more Facebook friends than most, everyone knew him in his campus fellowship group and in any given week he had multiple opportunities to hang out with people who encouraged his faith. He loved his major and student teaching placement. He dreamed of the ways he could use his degree to make a difference in the lives of inner-city kids (think *Dangerous Minds* or *Freedom Writers*). But Curt quickly discovered that "they weren't going to make a major motion picture about [his] life teaching students." In fact, the day his evaluator from Teach for America came to offer performance feedback, his classroom was in complete disarray, and one of his male students ran up behind the female supervisor and started air-grinding. Curt remembers another moment when it took everything in him not to scream an expletive at his students. He stood in front of the classroom with the f-word on the tip of his tongue, but instead of shouting he walked to the sink, gathered himself and went back to teaching. He held it together for that day. Overall, though, he was ready to throw in the towel.

Looking back it's easier to see how an experience like this can build character and shape us for good, but while we're in the thick of it we can quickly become frustrated, jaded or hopeless. *How do we maintain a healthy perspective in the midst of life's trials? How do we prepare and persevere?*

Your transition out of college may be nothing like Curt's; however, none of us gets through life without facing hardship. The twenties are some of the most exciting years, but there will also be hard days. Though life is not all fight, until Christ returns in full glory it is a battle. When we fail to realize this, it's like we run naked into open fire. We need to be armed with proper perspective and appropriate coping mechanisms to fight the good fight. We should anticipate struggles, learn how to persevere with virtue and trust that God has a purpose within them.

RETHINKING OUR RIGHT TO A "NORMAL" LIFE

Why are we often unprepared to handle adversity? As we consider our attitude toward adversity and our ability to persevere, it's important to understand the ways in which our culture has influenced us to pursue comfort and avoid pain. At every turn we get the message that peace, ease and efficiency matter most. We're told we must be doing something wrong or that we lack a certain consumer good if we don't feel happy and safe all the time. We live in the age of life hacks—where everyone is looking for a shortcut to make life easier and more productive. But what if these values counter those of Jesus and his kingdom? What if we're not meant to be comfortable all the time? What is a "normal" life for a Christ-follower? When we "seek to define 'normal' as freedom from all hardship" we may be undermining our humanness and failing to dignify the life Christ intends. [1]

One recent alum had the rest of her life mapped out before she finished college. Kristen planned to earn a degree in nutrition with a focus on global health and move to an underdeveloped country in Africa as a missionary. Shortly after she arrived in Gabon, she started experiencing significant health issues, which forced her to come back to the United States to seek more involved treatment. Eventually doctors discovered that Kristen had a rare and serious neurological condition called Chiari. The effects had reached the point of threatening her daily functioning, but the only option to relieve her symptoms involved a risky operation. After much prayer Kristen opted for surgery. Though the procedure went better than expected, Kristen is not out of the woods. She continues to battle other, seemingly unrelated, health issues and does not yet have answers to what's going on with her body.

As she reflects on all that she's been through in the last few years, Kristen says, "I really think the overarching lesson this whole time has been about my expectations of how life should be. I also think I had the idea that God owed me. That if I lived a good life, God owed me a good life." Though her plans to serve overseas may defy many people's idea of comfort, Kristen still pictured living a "normal" life, free of unresolved health problems. A life where she could do what she wanted, unencumbered by her body's failure to respond in the way she would like or need.

Perhaps, like Kristen, we have certain expectations of how life should go. We need to consider:

- What is our definition of normal? What is a good life?

- How has our upbringing or culture shaped the way we view adversity?

- When trials come, do we know how to endure them with fortitude?

Our upbringing, affluence and cultural pressure to focus on personal gratification affect the way we approach hard times. Also, there are certain things about college that often don't prepare us for challenging stretches. Penn State's campus newspaper surveyed six student columnists with the question, "What is the greatest problem of your generation?" Half of them responded with something along these lines: *our sense of entitlement.*[2] We want things to go our way. And when one little thing doesn't play out as planned, we grumble, whine or fly off the handle.

For example, I will spend a day on campus listening to students complain about how frustrated they are because they dropped their cell phone and the face cracked, or they had to wait in line for an *hour* to renew their ID card, or it's calling for rain on their birthday. Then in the evening I go to my life group, made up of people who have been out of college for more than a decade, and there is a contrast in conversation. I hear prayer requests from a married couple who cannot conceive a child, or for a friend who birthed a stillborn baby, or for a brother who's incarcerated. This is not to say that I don't have conversations with college students dealing with significant pain or that people over thirty (myself included) don't complain about shallow things; but more often than not I observe pretty thin skin among many students, causing me to be concerned for how they will handle the adversity that will come after graduation.

TAKE UP YOUR CROSS

Trials may tempt us toward apathy, avoidance or self-loathing, but these are not the coping mechanisms God intends. Instead he invites us to take up our cross daily and to not be surprised by struggles (Luke 9:23; John 16:33). The Christian life is not a prevention plan against hard times, but it does provide a framework for guiding our response in the midst of them. In fact, the Bible tells us that we should expect to "face trials of many kinds" and "consider it pure joy" when we do (James 1:2). We're called to *rejoice* in suffering because "our present sufferings are not worth comparing with the glory that will be revealed in us" (Romans 8:18). This is our armor for adversity.

When was the last time you heard a sermon on the sheer joy of suffering? Or on the importance of taking up your cross daily? Too often the church caters to our culture, and in an effort to be attractive we sometimes weaken the gospel message. When we encounter the true gospel, we understand the *cost* involved in Christ going to the cross on our behalf. The gospel is this: our sin runs deeper than we can imagine, but grace runs even deeper. When we come to terms with the depths of our depravity, the cross enlarges in our life, and our eyes open to the cost as well as the sweetest reward possible: forgiveness of our sin and unity with Christ for now and all eternity! Our gratitude for this reward should fuel lives of worship that say yes to Jesus at every turn, even when it costs us everything.

One recent alum, Lucy, confesses she had been focusing on her own satisfaction rather than God's sanctifying work in her. Desperate to stay in the same city as her boyfriend while he finished graduate school, she applied for jobs there and trusted it would all work out. But it didn't. She didn't get the offer she hoped and took a job in another location. Reflecting on this initial disappointment, Lucy says, "I'm really thankful God showed me that I can't hold on to my plans really tightly. It's not so much about trusting in the Lord that he had a better job in mind for me, but trusting that what matters is my sanctification, my heart change. *Jesus* is the better thing." Her plan did not work out, but Lucy has grown in her relationship with Jesus, her relationship with her boyfriend and her ability to live with open hands.

When we can see our present sufferings, disappointments and trials as a means of shaping our hearts to be better followers of Jesus in this life and for all eternity, our perspective changes and we grow in our ability to endure. It's hard to keep this mindset in the midst of struggles, but we must remember that people will watch to see how we handle trials. Our character in the face of adversity may be the greatest witness to Christ and his coming kingdom that we have to offer others.

By saying we should jump for joy when we experience hardships, I in no way want to diminish the adversity you may be facing right now, the pain you feel or the trial that may be ahead. Nor do I want to minimize the suffering you may have already endured. While there are certain things about college that do not prepare us for suffering, there are experiences *during* college that do. I've walked with many students who have faced real hardship in college (or who have chosen to deal with pain from their past while in college): their parents' divorce, a loved one's sickness, a battle with an eating disorder, the death of a classmate or the desire to end their own life. These students were willing to be vulnerable with their Christian community and friends, to seek help from trusted mentors and, for some, to pursue professional counseling. The decision to face these trials head-on and to walk through them with others speaks to the bravery of these individuals. The way they have undergone trials in college will undoubtedly shape them for facing future hardship.

Whether our trials occur before, during or after college, we need to call them what they are, not have some Pollyanna attitude or offer

Christian platitudes in the face of deep struggle and pain. At the same time, let's never diminish the gospel truth. Even as we wait for relief from our suffering, we serve a God who is at work in the midst of it. In adversity he is near, bringing about the *good* of those who love him (Romans 8:28). Nothing can separate us from him or from Christ's love (Romans 8:35). Our troubles allow us to cling to Christ—maybe like never before—as they refine and prove our faith. When we choose to take up our cross daily, our trials show us and others our true reward: Jesus.

There are many aspects of suffering that we cannot adequately address here (why does God allow it, the problem of evil, God's sovereignty), but it is important to emphasize that pain and trials are an inevitable part of life in a broken world. We cannot escape this world, but we can choose *how* we will live while we're here.

BEAR ONE ANOTHER'S BURDENS

Though the process of enduring our present suffering requires deep personal faith, we are not meant to go through life's trials alone. Whether this means reaching out to our community rather than retreating in times of suffering or stepping into someone else's struggle, the apostle Paul calls us to carry each other's burdens (Galatians 6:2) and to mourn with those who mourn (Romans 12:15). When we're at our lowest point, inviting someone else to come alongside us may be the hardest thing to do, but God calls us to let others in.

In walking with many alums through difficult times, I'm not sure I've seen two people reach out to their community the way Mark and Hannah did during the nightmare they recently lived. They met in our college ministry, got married on a gorgeous fall day, and a few months after their one-year anniversary found out they were expecting their first child. Then came devastating news. The baby was not developing properly. Testing revealed a rare genetic defect that caused kidney malfunction, heart problems and an encephalocele or small opening at the base of the skull, among other issues. If Hannah carried the child to full term, he would likely not survive.

I remember the day Mark shared the heartbreaking news. The doctors informed them that they had two options: terminate or wait for the baby to die on his own. They made the personal choice to continue the pregnancy, saying "God has a purpose for our baby, and while it might not be a long-term purpose, it is his decision to take the baby or not."

As Hannah's stomach grew with child, the gravity of the situation weighed heavily. Week after week they learned more negative information about their baby. Throughout the pregnancy Mark faithfully updated our community, and they both continued to be a part of church life. Months before their due date, Hannah and Mark made the brave decision to stand before our congregation and have their unborn baby, Josiah Emmanuel, formally dedicated to God (a public ceremony for parents to offer their child to God and express their desire to raise him in the faith).

Hannah carried Josiah to full term, welcomed him into the world and held him with Mark for ninety-five minutes before Josiah died in their arms. At Josiah's funeral service Mark read the eulogy he wrote for his son, baring his soul as he shared his anger, confusion and grief. At the same time, he displayed unwavering faith and hope. As others shared from up front, a theme emerged: "the life and ministry of Josiah Emmanuel." Because of how Mark and Hannah endured this trial, a child who lived for only ninety-five minutes has made a difference in the kingdom in ways no one will fully know.

Throughout this deep trial, Mark and Hannah chose to let others in—to all of it. The mess, the anger, the questions, the pain. They let their lives and the life of their child minister to others. Seeing their faith inspired us to find deeper faith of our own. Watching them love each other made us want to love our spouses and others better. Mark and Hannah have said that they could not imagine walking through this without their community. We—who have been changed in ways we'll never forget—couldn't imagine it either.

POSTURES AND PRACTICES FOR
PERSEVERING THROUGH ADVERSITY

Life after college will have trials. We cannot change this reality, but we can choose how we will deal with current hardships or with past adversities that may resurface during the vulnerable time of being in transition. We practice perseverance in the many moments that precede the trial itself—by training our heart and choosing postures that will help us endure with virtue.

Practice fortitude. Fortitude is "the strength of mind that enables a person to . . . bear pain or adversity with courage."[3] If we want to suffer well, we need grit. We need to be tough in mind and spirit. As Christians, practicing fortitude often means that we acknowledge our weakness and helplessness before God and we allow him to be our strength. The ability to endure ultimately comes from him (2 Corinthians 12:9).

Despite suffering the year from hell, Curt kept his teaching commitment (although he did research Bible verses about keeping oaths to see whether he could get out of it!). Things did not miraculously improve in that year or even in the next. Curt remembers feeling trapped, alone and in despair much of those years. He'll never forget the dread that welled up each time he drove away from a weekend visiting his family, knowing he had to return to his isolated life. But Curt kept on. His faith in Christ sustained him, and in the end he found out what he was made of. He's not sure how he mustered the strength, but he chose to read a chapter of the Bible each day. He also had two or three key verses for every day of the week, trusting that if he read the "Monday verses" fifty-two times in a year he'd eventually memorize and *live* them. These spiritual disciplines were not a magic pill, but they were a crucial part of practicing fortitude in the face of adversity. Though Curt would never choose to repeat those first couple of years out of college, the experience became a significant part of his story, building character in him and growing his trust in God.

Similarly, for Kristen mental strength involved meditating on truth. She says, "The biggest thing is to preach the gospel to myself: I'm more sinful than I can imagine, and more loved than I could dare hope. My physical condition has nothing to do with what I do or what I have done." Kristen had to learn that her symptoms are not a punishment for sin, nor are her "right behaviors" going to heal her. "It's all about who he is. He really is with us, always. He never leaves us." As we focus on truth, we can also ask the Spirit to arrest our negative thoughts as quickly as they come. We can choose to face each day and its demands rather than worrying about things down the road that we cannot control or letting our mind spiral into a scenario that doesn't even exist.

Our fortitude is tested in difficulties, but it's built in the day to day—like the time Curt chose to suppress his anger with his students and practice self-control instead. When we decide to remain calm in traffic or not complain when we pick the longest line at the grocery store, we practice virtue. These little moments prepare our hearts for handling hard times.

Choose community. It's hard to reach out to others when we're not doing well ourselves. This challenge is often compounded right after college when we're still trying to build community or reestablish ourselves in a former one. We're often taught that needing others signifies weakness; we don't want to burden others with our stuff, and we may not want to be bothered by someone else's. But in the midst of adversity we need others most—people who will carry us and place us before Jesus when we don't have strength on our own (Mark 2:1-12).

How do we do this in a transitional time? It may mean reaching out to a former mentor or college friend until we've established new relationships. It may require being vulnerable with new people God has placed in our path. It may mean being there for someone else, even though we're dealing with our own struggles. Reaching out may involve all of these, at the same time.

Embrace small starts. Our lives don't have to be perfect or grand for them to be good. The prophet Zechariah warns us to not dare despise the day of small beginnings (Zechariah 4:10). Life is about small starts and magnificent finishes. Let's keep this in mind as we think about what we wish could be going better or who we wish we could be, remembering that God is at work even as we long for more.

Curt was far from being a shining star in his first job, but he made a commitment and stuck it out. In fact, as his time came to a close he contemplated continuing in Baltimore with the incredible students he had met. His experiences laid the foundation for future steps. Curt decided to move back to his hometown and was offered a job in one of the most highly rated districts in the state. Because of what he endured during his "year from hell," Curt was the least stressed teacher in the district in his next job. While others complained about students who shouted out the answers too often or scheduling woes that cut into their only free time, Curt sailed. Their concerns seemed minor compared to what he had undergone in his previous position and personal life.

Wait well. Every one of us is waiting for something—for a better job, for a relationship, for a conflict to resolve, for an answer to our deepest prayer, for the kingdom to fully come on earth as it is in heaven. If all of life is a waiting time, let's dedicate ourselves to waiting well—to practicing patience, giving thanks and accepting that God's ways are not our ways (Isaiah 55:8).

In an effort to wait better, my friend Cheryl gave up complaining one year during Lent (the forty days that precede Easter). Each time she complained, she added an extra day to her fast. By the time she reached Easter, she joked that she probably needed to extend her commitment until Christmas! Though an imperfect attempt, this practice began to build a heart reflex within her. How would our waiting look different if we chose to fast from complaining (even for a day, a week or forty days)? Or how might our hearts change if we replaced our grumbling with gratitude? What if we took on a challenge as author Ann Voskamp did, making a list of one thousand gifts, finding countless ordinary things to be thankful for even in the midst of hardship?[4]

As we wait, the most important thing we can do is fix our eyes on Jesus. Pastor and theologian A. W. Tozer defined faith as "the gaze of the soul upon a saving God."[5] When we direct our eyes toward Jesus and off of our circumstances, it changes us. As we train our "inward eyes" to behold God, our temporal sufferings become "scenes of this passing world"—we view them differently in light of a greater reality.[6]

In a recent article, Wesley Hill, a Christian gay man committed to celibacy, points to this greater view.[7] He opens by comparing two of his female friends. Both of them desire marriage and are committed to traditional Christian ethics on sexuality, believing "the marriage of a man and a woman is the only God-ordained place for sexual intimacy."[8] The difference between these friends: one is gay. At age fifty, Hill's straight friend recently admitted that her dream of marriage may not come true anytime soon. His gay friend also longs for intimacy with a partner but chooses to give this up; "because she's gay, she feels that marriage to a man is not in the cards . . . and marriage to another woman is not something she can consider." While discussing the ways the Christian faith community can honor (instead of shame) LGBT individuals who choose celibacy, Hill makes a larger point: the burdens we're asked to shoulder in this lifetime—sacrifices we may never choose for ourselves—will be "remembered and rewarded" in heaven. Hill reminds us that no matter what cross we're called to carry, we can bear that burden with eternity in mind—the place of our ultimate reward.

As we face trials, let's fix our eyes on Jesus—the one who came to earth as the suffering servant. Giving up the position and comfort of heaven, Jesus stepped out of his rightful place, lowered himself and became one of us (Philippians 2). He endured the excruciating road to his crucifixion and was nailed to the cross he carried. Let us never forget that because of what Christ has done on that cross we are united with him, and our suffering in this life only prepares us for knowing him more deeply and for all eternity (2 Corinthians 4:16-18).

GOING DEEPER

1. Describe a time when you faced a difficult circumstance. How did you respond in the midst of it?

2. What are your typical coping mechanisms when things don't go as planned? Be honest.

3. What does it mean to have a theology of suffering? How will this make a difference during a time of transition?

4. What is the role of community in suffering? What can you do to better invite others into your life or to come alongside others in their trials?

5. How can you prepare for adversity? What is one practice or heart attitude you want to continue and one you want to work on to help you respond well to adversity?

6. How can you fix your eyes on Jesus and eternity in the midst of trials?

Scripture study: Isaiah 55:8; Romans 8; Romans 12:15; 2 Corinthians 12:9; 2 Corinthians 4:16-18; Philippians 2; James 1:2

Recommended reading:

Michael Card, *A Sacred Sorrow* (Colorado Springs: NavPress, 2005).

Timothy Keller, *Walking with God Through Pain and Suffering* (New York: Dutton, 2013).

Ben Palpant, *A Small Cup of Light* (Mud&Spit Enterprises, 2014).

FOUR

THE TYRANNY OF CHOICE

MAKING GOD-HONORING DECISIONS

*Our failure to hear His voice when we want to is due to
the fact that we do not in general want to hear it, that
we want it only when we think we need it.*

DALLAS WILLARD, *HEARING GOD*

FROM WHETHER TO WAKE UP with our alarm or press snooze to what to eat for breakfast to how to organize our time, daily life is chock-full of choices.[1] And this doesn't include those big life decisions we must make, especially when transitioning out of college. From the small to the big, it's often difficult to lead ourselves in making good choices. Sometimes it would be nice if someone else would just decide for us, right? In some ways we are blessed to have a multitude of options available to us, but on the other hand it can be paralyzing. How do we choose?

In my first year out of college I worked with youth on probation. Some of them had previously spent time in correctional programs or psychiatric facilities, and though it may sound strange, some almost longed to go back—not because they liked being in trouble but because there, nearly every decision had been made for them. Going from a situation where someone else basically decided when you could use the bathroom to normal life and all its demands was totally overwhelming.

Entering life after college comes with similar challenges, especially because it is *filled* with decisions:

- Where should I live?
- Should I apply for graduate school or enter the job market?
- Which job offer should I accept?
- Should I continue the dating relationship I started in college? Move to the same city as my boyfriend/girlfriend? Get engaged?
- How do I pursue my own path with the pressures of pleasing my parents?

I'm not sure that I can help make a hard decision any easier, but I can offer some perspective, principles and tools for the process—because decision making is a *process*. Before we can begin the steps of basic biblical decision making, it's best to understand some big-picture principles as well as the larger grid that guides us.

WHAT WE ARE UP AGAINST: THE WAY THE WORLD MAKES DECISIONS

I spent the summer before my senior year of college in Chifeng, China—a city of beauty, history and *one* brand of laundry detergent. After returning to the United States, I had a near breakdown in the laundry detergent aisle of the grocery store as I surveyed the landscape of choices. Tide? Wisk? All? Bounty? Ultra Bounty? Ultra Bounty with bleach alternative . . . you get my point. Paralyzed by the wall of washing products, the smells swirling together, my head started spinning and I broke into a sweat. I wanted to run back to China and select The White Cat—the one and only laundry detergent choice. Faced with so many options, I became overwhelmed to the point of walking away empty-handed. Though I'm sure my experience was a combination of analysis paralysis and culture shock, we cannot deny the effect of the tyranny of choice. On nearly every front, we have more options today than at any other time in history. Though I celebrate this progress, the multitude of options may also be killing us.

When paralyzed by a sea of choices, we often shut down and cannot decide. So we don't. Sadly, this happens with decisions that are far more significant than our laundry detergent. We maintain the status quo, avoid tough decisions or choose apathy. None of these is helpful or biblical. Neither is the reverse approach—instead of doing nothing, some people choose to try anything; if you can't decide or you fear missing out, just opt for whatever grabs you at that moment, whatever you *feel* like.

I met with a graduating senior, Theresa, who had a serious struggle with decision making. She often found herself making poor choices and had a difficult time discerning why. Theresa attended church, met with our fellowship group and showed up to our discipleship times, but when it came to making healthy choices in between those meetings, she continually struggled. Reflecting on her weekend decisions to hang out at a club with a friend who she admitted was not the best influence, drink too much and end up in a compromising situation with a guy, Theresa said, "I just don't know how I got there."

After digging deeper, she eventually realized how much her choices were influenced by her mom's advice and the cultural message YOLO (You Only Live Once). Theresa had been raised by a mother whose primary guiding principle in making most decisions was "Why not?" When Theresa faced a decision, she almost always talked to her mom about it because she was so used to asking for her advice on everything. When her mom grew tired of Theresa's questions, "sometimes she'd brush [them] off with her 'why not' approach." Leading with this advice and her current emotions, Theresa's default was to just "go for it"—even when it brought devastating consequences. It is hard to unlearn the things we have been taught by our parents, and it doesn't help when the culture reinforces our bad practices.

We live in a culture where emotion-based decision making is the norm. If it feels right, just go for it. And if it doesn't feel good, it must not be right. Culturally we seek pleasure and avoid pain. Allowing our emotions to drive our decision making is far from what God intends. He doesn't want us to over-spiritualize every choice we make (should I eat a hoagie or pizza for lunch?), but he desires for us to seek him in our decision making. We need to be aware of the ways our culture and family of origin have shaped our decision making patterns, and we need to look to God's best for this area of our lives.

WHAT IS GOD'S WILL FOR MY LIFE?

Applying God's Word and wisdom to our choices is a key part of biblical decision making, but if we're honest, we admit this is not easy. The Scriptures are complicated and so are our circumstances. Regarding a tough choice (Should I accept a job offer in a better location but with a 50 percent pay cut? Should I marry this person and enter into a covenant with them for life?) God's Word is often not cut and dry. It would be great if we could flip the pages of our Bibles roulette-style, open to a random passage, apply it to our situation and call it biblical decision making. But God's revelation of himself through his Word doesn't work like this.

When we question how to apply the Bible to our decision making, I think what we're really asking is *What is God's will for my life? What does he want me to do in this situation?* When it comes to discerning God's will, sometimes we overcomplicate it. Some of us become so consumed by wanting to make the just-right choice that we agonize over every major (and minor) life decision. We wrongly view the discernment process like target practice, trying desperately to hit the bull's-eye—otherwise we'll be demoted forever to permanent plan B. We wring our hands, go over scenarios again and again, and plead for God to reveal each detail of his perfect plan.

While some obsess over every choice, others may assume that God takes little interest in our decisions. We may question, *Does God have a plan for my life? Does he really care whether I take this job or that one? Is God invested in what I do?* Viewing him as an uninvolved, unconcerned deity is not biblical. Nor is seeing him as a god who plays hide and seek, hoping we'll find him and his right plan otherwise he'll doom us. He doesn't set our lives in motion, sit back and then see whether we'll mess them up, nor is he waiting to screw us over if we don't pick his perfect plan.

On a very basic level, God's will is for us to love him, love others and partner in his kingdom work. Making a healthy choice can be as simple as deciding to join God where he's already working, or asking, Does this decision allow me to love God and others? We don't need to overcomplicate it.

For example, when faced with a choice whether to accept an offer to work for a nonprofit organization, despite some pressure from her parents to either move back home or secure a higher-grossing job, Chelsea says, "Taking the job at the Pregnancy Resource Clinic was honestly sort of a no-brainer." After a summer of job shadowing in her field, occupational therapy, Chelsea had come back to school realizing that she didn't want to pursue that line of work, but she was uncertain about her future. During that same summer Chelsea spent a significant amount of time with her sister, who had just had an unplanned pregnancy. This experience led Chelsea to start volunteering at the Pregnancy Resource Clinic when she got back to school. In November of her senior year, Chelsea began praying for an opportunity to work at the clinic. God answered that prayer by opening a position three weeks after graduation. When Chelsea considered her past experiences and her current passions, she saw God at work. Being able to see God's hand in the situation and "where he had been working all along" made it easy to accept the position despite other pressures. She didn't need to overthink it.

HOW DO I KNOW WHETHER I'M IN GOD'S WILL?

Sometimes we wrongly assume that God has this ideal, hidden blueprint that we must decode at every turn in order to live faithfully. The Bible does not teach that God has some secret "individual will" for us, but it does show that God has a sovereign and moral will.[2] God is ultimately in control of everything; nothing happens that it is outside of his plan. This doesn't mean that God *causes* all things to happen but that he allows them. God does have a plan for us, and "the events and choices of [our lives] . . . work that plan into detail."[3] Though we cannot fully unpack the complexity of our freedom and God's control, simply put, as God guides we choose what he has planned.

Though we may not know God's ultimate plan until something has already unfolded, we do know his moral will—or his "will of desire."[4] Through his Word God has revealed commands for us to follow so we can pursue obedience and holiness. Often we obsess over decisions that are non-moral (such as which job to take) while caring too little about whether we're living as we ought to in other areas (such as how we treat money, sex, each other or any part of the creation).[5] When we make decisions that are outside God's desires, we feel the effects of our poor choices and will be held accountable, but God's ultimate will prevails. In all things we should aim to live morally, trusting God has a sovereign plan.

How does this work in the big decisions of our daily lives? Let's say you've received a job offer to work at the headquarters of a competitive company in the field you've trained in. It's a great opportunity, but it will involve a move across the county. You love the vision and values of the company, you'll get some incredible training and you anticipate you'll enjoy the work. Your other option is to work for a small, local company near your hometown. The small staff and limited scope make it less appealing, but the plus side is that you can stay close to family and the person you've been dating for the last two years.

This decision is not easy, but it can be less stressful if you know that taking the offer at the large company or leaving it doesn't mean you're in or out of the "center of God's will"—a phrase that is not biblical or helpful. If an option is not morally wrong (as in this case), and it allows us to love God and others (arguably true in either scenario), then it's likely that we can freely choose without fear. As we pray and seek to make the best decision, we may ask:

- Do I sense an internal pull or calling toward one or the other?

- Do others sense one decision would be better than another?

- What do I want to do?

As we face tough decisions, it's important to know that in many cases God graciously allows us to choose between two or more *good* options. So let's caution ourselves against any approach to decision making that stacks equally good choices on top of one another like rings in a target. God cares what we choose because he loves us, but he's not going to cast us into some parallel universe if we pick one good option over the other!

CAN I MESS UP GOD'S WILL FOR MY LIFE?

As we seek to make the best choice we can, we may question, *Can I mess up God's will? What if I'm distracted and I don't notice the person I'm supposed to marry? What if I take the wrong job offer and move to the wrong city? What if . . .* If we think of our lives as some linear progression from one thing to the next, then it's natural that we'll wonder whether we are on the right track to that next thing. But I'd argue that this is not how God works. As of right now I can tell you with clarity that I feel God has led me to my occupation, location, spouse and role as a mother; however, when I look back on my life the progression to this point has been far from linear. My experiences have been more of a mess of dots that God has graciously connected as he has worked out his will. The experiences of heartbreak, loss, career indecision and rejection did not make me feel like I was moving forward with God's plan for my life; however, it has been those very seasons of struggle, uncertainty and spiritual wilderness that have shaped me. I believe these were all a part of God's plan at the time, and he has used them for good and will continue to use them for his future plan.

So even when we blatantly disobey, choose something that is outside of God's moral will or live with a passive indifference toward God, we are not going to mess up his plan. If we repent and return to him he will still work out his plan. It may not be our plan, but woe to us if we think we are powerful enough to mess it up! The God of the universe guides us; surely his leadership in our lives trumps our feeble attempts to know and do his will.

Though it's possible to make decisions that are not God's best for us, we serve a God who can—and does—redeem our bad choices. Abraham was called to leave his father's house, kindred and everything familiar to go to an unknown place. Well, guess what? He was not fully obedient. He took Lot, his nephew, with him (Genesis 12:5), which brought them both much grief along the way; he lied before the Egyptians about his wife, Sarah, telling them she was his sister, which brought disgrace on him and almost resulted in Sarah being taken to bed by Pharaoh (Genesis 12:11-20); and when he believed God was slow in keeping his promise, Abraham agreed to sleep with Sarah's servant, Hagar, with hopes of fulfilling the promise on his own (Genesis 16). More grief and misery followed. In all of these acts of disobedience, God continued to see Abraham's repentant heart and strong faith. God did not give up on him, redeemed his poor decisions and never backed down on keeping his promise. This is the sovereign God we serve.

Despite our circumstances and difficult decisions, internal peace within the process is a promise of a life with Christ (Philippians 4:7). At the same time, I'm not sure we always get what some call a sense of peace when we make a good choice, especially initially. I know recent graduates who have chosen to obey God kicking and screaming (especially when God called them out of something—out of a relationship they wanted to hold on to or out of a familiar place to go somewhere unknown). In the beginning these alumni felt more chaos than peace, but in retrospect they can honestly say that God knew exactly what he was doing and that choosing obedience was for their best.

On the flip side, I know many alumni who have made peace with decisions that are far from God's best for them (such as decisions to live with their boyfriend or girlfriend, quit going to church or stop tithing). Like the prophet Jonah peacefully asleep in the boat after blatantly disobeying God, these alumni rationalize and settle in to their poor choices. Let us choose to live in grace, knowing that we will mess up, but let's never grab for cheap grace: purposely turning away from God's best in hopes that he will forgive us.

SO *HOW* DO I MAKE DECISIONS?

Attuning ourselves to God.[6] Before we delve into a step-by-step process for decision making, we must discuss a crucial prestep: cultivating our daily relationship with Christ. If we are going to make wise decisions that honor God, then we need to pursue a close relationship with him. We must attune ourselves to him—his character, thoughts, precepts and promises. Aligning ourselves with God's frequency in everyday relationship with him will prepare us to listen and discern in the big decisions. Though God is always near, it takes time and patience for us to attune ourselves to him. We can't expect to hear from God instantly when we haven't worked to cultivate a relationship with him, nor can we expect to easily start the practices of prayer or Scripture study when a big decision comes. We should start now if we're not already in the habit and continue if we are. The choices we make in the big decisions are born in many little decisions. Most often, a good or poor choice starts not with that particular decision but with the many that preceded it. We need to get into the practice of making wise choices in the small things, so we are better equipped for the decision-making process later.

A step-by-step process. In his book *Step by Step* James Petty describes a process for biblical decision making. Key steps in the process include (1) consecration, (2) information, (3) supplication and (4) consultation.[7] All of these steps prepare us to make an actual decision.

Consecration. When faced with a difficult decision, we must first decide whether we are willing to give the decision and ourselves fully to God. Like Abraham laying down his own son Isaac on the altar, we must decide to place everything before God. Consecrating ourselves means that we declare our life and situation as sacred—as something that fully belongs to God. According to Petty, "The first step in seeking guidance from God is to ask him to test and search our hearts for any areas of life, belief or motives that are not given over to him."[8] As the Holy Spirit reveals, we must confess, repent and continue to let him guide.

When one recent alum, Jackie, was trying to decide about making a major move to a new city (Denver) she confessed, "I wasn't really sure if I was making this move based on my own wants or God's desire, so I just kept praying about it." As she continued to pray, she also kept "trying to put God into every aspect" of the decision. When Denver continued to come up in conversations with a friend she considered moving with (someone she knew would encourage her in her walk with Christ), with her family or seemingly at random, Jackie considered, "maybe God really is moving here." Wanting to make sure she was fully giving the decision to him, Jackie continued to pray and lay her life before God.

Information. Before making any major decision, it's important to understand as much about it as possible. "We need information about ourselves, the others involved, potential consequences, responsibilities, and of course, circumstances."[9] We should never dismiss the basic God-given faculty of our brain with its ability to gather useful information and logically process aspects of the decision. We shouldn't be afraid to ask questions—and thereby seek answers—before we commit to an option. If we're thinking of taking a new job, we can talk with current employees who can illuminate more about the corporate culture. If we're moving to a new location, we can research potential housing areas and local church options. If we're considering moving overseas for missions, we can learn about the new people group and the opportunities and obstacles for the gospel there. All of these can be helpful in gathering information that will allow us to discern the situation.

As Jackie considered two good options before her—staying in her hometown, close to family, or moving to Denver—she kept getting "this itching feeling . . . like it was time to do something new." As Jackie and her friend gathered information about Denver, they looked into cost of living, transportation options and the job market. The huge population of young professionals there—a significant fact they learned—pushed them closer to making the move. As Jackie continued to ask God and others for wisdom, she and her friend eventually decided to head to Denver. Though some of her friends questioned Jackie's decision to move without a job offer, in the end Jackie believed it was God's leading and she trusted him with the details. Shortly after she moved, God provided in an incredible way: he opened doors for her to obtain a competitive nurse assistant job at a hospital (which usually hires only applicants with extensive experience or internal connections) within ten minutes walking distance from her apartment! She could not be more thankful for God's hand in the job and her move.

When faced with two genuinely good options, info gathering can be a key step in helping you decide which to choose. Sometimes it may come down to knowing yourself and your personal desires. The basic question of *What do I want?* is not invalid or unspiritual. However, it's also important to keep in mind that just because an opportunity presents itself, it doesn't mean we must go in that direction. Even a good option may not be the best decision.

For example, I know two recent alumni who met each other in the context of work when they were assigned to the same team. They developed a friendship and then began pursuing each other for a possible dating relationship. All of the signs seemed to point to "go for it." They both had interest and their actions showed great mutual respect for each other; however, when they started to pray about it they concluded that "just because it seems the door is open here, it doesn't mean we should walk through." They opted to remain friends and forgo the dating relationship—a decision neither of them regrets.

Supplication. Beyond just being willing to lay down our decision (consecration), God wants us to pray and ask him for specific direction. On one hand, we can become so fixated on "finding God's will" that we flounder in indecision, failing to move forward because we've over-spiritualized our choice.[10] But on the other hand, we sometimes place too much weight on our own ability to make decisions (or to do anything for that matter), when it's impossible for us to garner the wisdom we need without God. When we come to terms with this, we can submit ourselves and our situation to God for his leading rather than our own. In the supplication step we petition God for guidance. We invite him to give us the "Spirit of wisdom and revelation" for our situation (Ephesians 1:17), trusting him to deposit it through his Word, prayer and the Holy Spirit.

As we offer our decision to God, we may or may not receive a clear answer. It's crucial to persevere in prayer, knowing that our prayer life may be changing us more than anything else.

In the step of supplication one senior wanted to know, "How do you draw the line between not being passive but also not stressing out or not putting God in a box with regard to a timeline?" There's a distinct difference between passivity and trust. Though they may look similar from the outside, passivity is the mark of a heart that does not care. In contrast, a heart that trusts does not fret, perseveres and prays, even up to (and in!) the eleventh hour.

In his book The Best Question Ever,
*Andy Stanley claims that discerning life's
decisions comes down to one question:
"What is the wise thing to do?"*[11]

We cannot put God in a box or nail him down to a timeline even if we tried, but we can create artificial deadlines in decision making if we need to—or they may be in place for us, depending on the decision. For example, you may say, "I need to know by the end of this month whether I'm going to stay in this job or begin to pursue other options." We should submit our decision to God, petition him in prayer and also invite others to pray with us and for us. And then when the deadline comes we make the best decision we can based on our sense of God's leading.

Consultation. The book of Proverbs emphasizes the wisdom of inviting counselors or advisers into the decision-making process (Proverbs 11:14; 15:22). The consultation step encourages us to seek counsel from people who may be able to give insight into the entirety of the situation, especially older, wiser individuals with experience and spiritual discernment.

It's important to seek a number of counselors, but don't ask too many people. I know alumni who have too much pride to invite anyone into their decision-making process as well as others who cannot make a decision without asking every family member, mentor, friend and stranger for their opinion. Neither extreme is healthy or helpful. We should humble ourselves enough to receive counsel from others (maybe three or four people), but we should not allow everyone and anyone to speak into our situation to the point of confusing us. One other pitfall: we should avoid asking only those who will affirm what we've already decided. Sometimes we make up our minds and then go through the motions of asking someone's advice when we really don't want it. If we want to honor God, we should take this step seriously, humbling ourselves before God and others, and then go from there.

Summary. As we come before God in the steps of consecration, information, supplication and consultation, we prepare our hearts and minds for making a decision. All of these work together to inform our decision:

- prayer
- Scripture
- spiritual counsel
- common sense
- previous experience
- personal desires
- circumstances

As we do our best to apply a decision-making process to our lives, we must also release ourselves and our decision to God once we make our choice. Many decisions involve a risk, and we need to be okay if things don't play out as we planned. Martina, an alum who took this process seriously, shares,

Don't be afraid of failure. . . . I applied to grad school a few years ago. It was something I had always wanted to do, I sought counsel, I saved some money, and then I took a risk. I got accepted and enrolled. Then when I took the first semester of classes, I realized I couldn't balance working full-time and getting a degree part-time. . . . I took a leave of absence after the first semester and haven't gone back. I don't regret trying it, and although I spent a few thousand dollars on the tuition, I don't think it was a bad or sinful decision. It was a good experience to try and I learned a lot about making decisions through the process.

Even if a decision seems like a *really big* decision, very few are as major as we make them out to be. Obviously moving to a large city, taking a new job and buying a house or car should all be taken seriously and are life-changing, but they aren't impossible to reverse. It's okay to make a decision that may not turn out as you hoped. It's also important to keep in mind that a yes to one thing may mean a no to another. Sometimes we say no to a good thing to say yes to a better thing, knowing we can't have it all—nor do we need it all. Decision making comes with obvious challenges. We should give ourselves grace and be patient with ourselves in the process. The very thing God wants to teach us may have nothing to do with the actual decision but rather with what we're learning in the process of making it.

In some of my biggest decisions (like choosing to accept a certain job offer, getting married, buying a home), I wanted God to appear as he did to Moses—flashy and unforgettable like the burning bush in the wilderness. I wanted certainty. I'd tell you it's because I wanted to honor God, but mostly I think I just didn't want to get it wrong. I wanted an "A" in decision making, to not mess up or make a mistake. In the search for God to drop the answer in my lap or write it in sky, I almost failed to see all the subtle ways he was showing himself to me. Though I may not have had certainty, countless little revelations have carried me to the decisions I've made, and I see his strong hand in all of it. My hope is that you too can choose to trust him, even in uncertainty. Most of all, may you have eyes to see and ears to hear the thousand ways he's revealing himself to you *right now*.

GOING DEEPER

1. What decisions are you facing right now?

2. How have you typically made decisions in the past? When it comes to the extremes of doing nothing (paralyzed by options so you cannot decide) and doing everything and anything (deciding based on what feels good at the time, the why-not? approach), do you tend to fall to one side or the other? Explain.

3. Do you believe God has a plan for your life? Why or why not?

4. What stood out to you about the step-by-step decision-making process?

5. Is there anything you would like to stop, continue or start doing when it comes to your decision-making process?

6. What is one thing you can do right now to apply a principle or practice to the decision(s) you are facing?

Scripture study: Proverbs 1:7; 11:14; 15:22; Jeremiah 6:16; Ephesians 1:17; Philippians 4:4-7

Recommended reading on hearing God and practicing his presence:
Brother Lawrence, *The Practice of the Presence of God* (New York: Revell, 1895).
Susan S. Philips, *The Cultivated Life: From Ceaseless Striving to Receiving Joy* (Downers Grove, IL: InterVarsity Press, 2015).
A. W. Tozer, *The Pursuit of God* (Minneapolis: Bethany House, 2013).
Dallas Willard, *Hearing God: Developing a Conversational Relationship with God* (Downers Grove, IL: InterVarsity Press, 1999).
Recommended reading on biblical decision making:
Kevin DeYoung, *Just Do Something: A Liberating Approach to Finding God's Will* (Chicago: Moody Publishers, 2009).

John Ortberg, *All the Places to Go: How Will You Know?* (Carol Stream, IL: Tyndale, 2015).

James Petty, *Step by Step: Divine Guidance for Ordinary Christians* (Phillipsburg, NJ: P&R, 1999).

PART TWO

REAL LIFE

FAITHFUL TO COMMUNITY

FIVE

BEYOND THE QUAD

FINDING FRIENDS

All the world's a stage,
And all the men and women merely players.
They have their exits and their entrances,
And one man in his time plays many parts.

WILLIAM SHAKESPEARE, *AS YOU LIKE IT*

MY BEST FRIEND GROWING UP WAS AIMÉE. She was my neighbor, playmate, tree-fort buddy and sleepover friend. Together we started mini entrepreneurial ventures on our street: everything from a lemonade stand to a gypsy moth caterpillar clean-up service. We created elaborate snow forts in the winter and performed original plays in the summer. Aimée came on my family's vacations, and we were at each other's birthday parties every year starting in second grade. We dreamed about our high school proms and wedding days. When our actual prom arrived, she's one of the few people who knew that I had a huge crush on the guy who took me. We were kindred spirits.

Then we went to college, in separate states. In the first few semesters I went to visit her and she came to see me. As we continued to meet new people, however, our visits and phone calls became less frequent. College changed me. College changed Aimée. I made new friends, and she did too. Our changing selves and environments forced us to renegotiate how we related. We both grieved for the way things used to be, but we also celebrated the new things God was bringing into our lives. Most importantly, we gave each other space to step into this new life season while staying connected in ways that worked for each of us. By recognizing that our friendship was changing, we allowed each other to transition.

I share this story to illustrate that our relationships will change after college, just as they did after high school. We will stay close with some college friends, we will lose touch with others and we may be surprised by which friends fall into which category. This may seems obvious, or it may seem impossible, but we will also make new friends—indeed, we must.

Though we live in a culture of the self-made individual and we highly value our independence, we need relationships. We may try to convince ourselves that we can do this life on our own, but we cannot. As one writer puts it, "Post-college life, with its independence, busyness, travel, romances, and domestic responsibilities, can trap anyone into self-absorption. . . . [It] is work to create space for friends. Even so, we don't need friendship *in spite* of all that's going on, but *because* of all that's going on."[1] We are made for community and companionship.

There are countless places in the Bible where we learn that God has created us for connection. We are made in the image of a God who is three persons in one. The Trinity is a model of the first community, and as the *imago Dei* (image of God) we reflect this innate characteristic. It was not good for Adam to be alone, so God made a companion for him. Jesus himself lived life with his twelve disciples and built his church with imperfect but interconnected people. The apostle Paul talks countless times about how we must do things for "one another":

love one another, be patient with one another, bear one another's burdens, serve one another, encourage one another. We cannot "one another" without others in our lives! We need each other.

Finding friends after college is crucial, but it may be one of the greatest challenges we face. In my talks with alumni this is *the* top struggle for most. One alum shares, "I was not prepared for the patience and intentionality it would take to make friends after college." Similar to other parts of the transition, the challenge often comes from a disconnect between our expectations and the reality we face. Because college is structured differently from the rest of life, the context for making friends changes significantly after graduation. Sheer proximity and daily access to people in the same life stage is perfect fodder for forging friendships, but when the geography of our lives changes our new setting may make it harder to cultivate meaningful relationships. Depending on our situation, it may be possible for us to go through an entire week without experiencing significant human interaction outside of work.

Students who attend commuter campuses or who move back to an established network at home may not experience the jarring effect of leaving a close-knit web of college relationships. If our primary community consists of family or friends we've kept since high school, then we may not have the same challenges as those who move to an entirely new location. That said, the friendship realm of our lives will still be in some flux. We may experience loss as certain friends move away while we stay put. Or we may struggle to reenter the fabric of friendships at home, especially as our friends may be "going in different directions, at different paces," as one alum who moved back home put it.

Regardless of our college experience and no matter what life stage we are in, we need to understand the shifting nature of friendship and how to prepare for change. We need to know how to be patient and purposeful, equipped with a mindset that welcomes others in even if it doesn't look like what we envision.

WHEN "ALL THE WORLD'S A STAGE," EXPECT CHANGE

I've heard someone use the opening image in Shakespeare's "All the world's a stage" monologue to help us understand the dynamic nature of friendship.[2]

> All the world's a stage,
> And all the men and women merely players.
> They have their exits and their entrances,
> And one man in his time plays many parts.[3]

This analogy—which compares the relational realm of our lives to a theatrical production—may be helpful as we anticipate how our friendships will change after college. During different scenes in our lives, people play different roles. God brings people in and out of our lives for unique purposes and in various ways at just the right time. There will be people who walk on stage in a role we need them to play as if on cue. Some of them will exit stage right or stage left, and we may never see them again, or they may unexpectedly reappear in a much later act. Some players will stay on stage with us for the better portion of our lives in a major role, while others have bit parts.

Regardless, it is no coincidence that all these players show up to play their parts at particular times. This can help us understand why people come and go in our lives, especially during transitional periods. We are dynamic people living in a dynamic world; therefore we are always redefining and renegotiating our relationships. Entrances and exits are all part of the production.

We may think there's no way we will lose touch with certain college friends, or that we will never form closer friendships than those forged during our undergraduate years. Though I cannot predict how you personally will navigate your college relationships beyond graduation, I can promise that you will change after college—and so will your friends. Our context also changes. The places and events that kept us and our friends close in college, such as Monday night Bible study or

Thursday wing night, cannot be counted on to draw us together in the same way. This is not good or bad. It just is.

We can and should grieve the loss of these special times and the unique experience of college life that allowed such friendships to form and flourish. If you are still in school, do your best to savor these last days with the friends you've made rather than counting down to the next thing! Through it all, may you also recognize and embrace the new opportunities God has in store.

CHOOSING TO TRANSITION

Though the individual who plays the part of our best friend during a certain time in our lives may change, our need for deep friendship remains the same. During all phases of our lives we need a friend who will "challenge the sins we have come to love, affirm the gifts we are afraid to claim and help us dream dreams we otherwise would not dream."[4] This is a person who remains loyal no matter what, loves us at our worst and pushes us toward our best—a soul friend.

Right after graduation, many of my soul friends were the people I had just done life with for the past four years. When I moved to an unknown town and found myself home alone on Friday and Saturday nights (something I wish I would have known to expect!), I called one of my college girls. If I wasn't calling them, it was because I was actually with them. I cannot count how many road trips I took in those first few months out of college to visit people with whom I felt loved and known. As I gallivanted off to different cities nearly every other weekend, I certainly wasn't putting down roots in my new location. I knew I needed to establish myself and start making friends, but every effort felt *tiring*. And with all of the other adjustments, I just wanted to be around people who were familiar.

Looking back, I know I needed those touch points with my close friends, but I also wish I would have pushed myself out of my comfort zone sooner. On those weekends I travelled, I wish I had made an effort to get back to town in time to attend the Sunday night meeting of twenty-somethings from the church I was checking out. When I was in town, I wish I had decided not to sleep through another morning worship service because I was tired and lonely and no one was going to notice whether I showed up or not. Thankfully, I forced myself out of bed enough times to eventually join that church and become a regular attendee; it's a place where I met some of my current closest friends.

But finding those friends didn't happen instantly, easily or organically. At first it meant staying in town. Then it required sitting through an awkward Bible study where one member, a single man two decades older than most of us, hijacked the conversation and talked for the duration about something entirely unrelated to the topic. We suffered through because we wanted what was on the other side: a time to talk to each other after the study ended. Really, it wasn't until we started hanging out afterward and in between that friendships formed—like when Beth suggested a few of the women grab dinner beforehand or when Brian asked us to help with a project for Habitat for Humanity. Though it took work, these initial time investments began to build on one another, making way for deeper conversation and, eventually, lasting friendship.

In those first few months after college, we desperately need meaningful connection and even face-to-face time (if possible) with friends who know our deepest heart. We should take a few road trips. Visit. Call. Cry. Laugh. Keep connected, *and at the same time* start to transition.

Transitions have been described as trapeze acts: in the same way a swinging trapeze artist grips a rung with one hand as he reaches out to the next, we too have one hand on the past as we reach out for the future. At some point, though, we have to fully engage that far rung. If we keep gripping tightly with both hands to the rung of our past, we will eventually lose our grip and fall. As we maintain a connection with the past, we must also learn to build real community in the present. We need to swing with the momentum of the transition, so we soar in our new location and beyond.

BEYOND HAPPY HOUR

In our search for real community, it may be tempting to find our primary social connection in ways that do not require as much effort, such as the "happy hour" subculture. I do not think it is wrong to have a drink (in moderation) with a coworker or even to approach happy hour as a starting ground for getting to know others, but if the bar scene becomes our sole venue for connection and community, we are missing God's best. When we are bored, lonely or simply in need of friendship, it is easy to settle for the lowest common denominator. One recent alum admits,

> It's so easy to get caught up in other forms of community like the drinking/bar/happy hour scene and things like that. . . . I'd definitely say before I got into the church, we were going out with coworkers on the weekends. I think that happens everywhere. . . . I still go out with my friends, but I see it differently now [that I have a church], and I approach it differently, especially the drinking part.

When such forms of community provide a low-hanging opportunity to find friends, it's not surprising so many alumni fall into this pattern. Walking with your coworkers from the office to a downtown bar is a breeze compared to forcing yourself out of bed on Sunday morning to check out a church where you will know no one. But let me plead with you to push yourself. It may not be comfortable or convenient, but it will be good. As another alum puts it, "There's only so much depth of conversation that comes from happy hour. . . . Finding friends outside of that context allows you to develop the vulnerability that's crucial for real relationships."

TAKING RISKS THAT LEAD TO REAL COMMUNITY

In a very practical sense, if we're going to make friends in our new city or town we need to *be* there. We need to commit to staying on the weekends and being present during the week—for office events, company outings or midweek small groups. It's easy to fall into a rhythm of going to work, heading home, eating dinner alone and binging on our favorite Netflix shows night after night. Not to downplay the importance of alone time, but we need friends, and we can choose to do something about that. Rather than waiting for friends to come our way, we can get off the couch and go after relationships. We can be intentional.

One alum, Ryan, who moved to a new location, says, "The people who are making friends are those who are being incredibly intentional. They are out doing things, out talking to people, and I decided to try the same thing. It's okay that you're not going to be friends with everybody, but that shouldn't stop you from staying 'hi' to a stranger." Ryan's relationships changed when he decided to put himself out there. He met friends through shared activities like playing volleyball and by joining the young professionals group at his church. While at these events, instead of "banking on someone spotting him and pulling him in" he took the ownership of introducing himself. It has made all the difference.

While those with outgoing personalities may be more drawn to putting themselves out there, introverts will need to figure out how to be intentional in ways more suited to their style. Introverts may need to focus more on socializing with a goal in mind, making friends with people who can connect them to others, looking for a role to play or finding a hobby.[5]

Dana is an introvert who stayed in the area of her alma mater after college. After almost a year of relying solely on an ever-dwindling friend group, she noticed that she had not reestablished a community. As more and more friends moved away, she says, "the empty space opened around me and I realized that for the first time since my freshman year in college I was going to have to go hunting for community."

How did Dana find friends? First, she joined ThirdPlace, the young professionals group at her church. Though she's never looked forward to large group functions, she opted to go because it served as a springboard to deeper relationships. She attended with "zero expectation of making an actual connection in that setting," but while there she looked to meet one or two people with whom she might enjoy grabbing a meal or coffee. She said her goal was to "get their contact information and set up a time to hang out in a setting where I'm comfortable." The more extroverted members welcomed her and introduced her to others; though these people did not become her closest friends, she said they "helped me find my person." She encourages introverts to value and leverage extroverts for the ways they help people connect.

The term "third place" comes from sociologist Ray Oldenburg, who believes that everyone needs a place outside of home and work to connect with others. ThirdPlace in State College formed when a recent graduate recognized the need for other young professionals to have a gathering place. If you can't find a third place, consider creating one!

In addition to her church community, Dana found rich relationships by pursuing a hobby: ballroom dancing. "A hobby gets you out in the world and doing, and it becomes an entry point for those who are lonely." She found people who shared her artistic passions through an outlet that provided a mental break from work and great exercise! It was easier to show up to an activity that she could almost hide behind than to put herself out there in a large social setting. Dana says, "Introverts feel like they belong when they have a few people who really get them, and that takes longer." She shared how important it was to give things time and give herself permission to possibly not have friends for a while. Dana also agrees that regardless of personality style, no one is exempt from the purposefulness required to make friends.

In addition to being purposeful and physically present at events where we can meet others, we need to be present in mind and spirit. With technology and our ability to connect with our best friends at any moment, it's tempting to stay in constant contact with people who know us. But this may come at the expense of really getting to know the people in our new location. Just because we *can* keep readily connected to all of our friends and family members doesn't mean we *should*—at least not with everyone.

Facebook and other forms of social media give the illusion that we can maintain relationships with countless individuals from all different scenes in our lives, but it's just that—an illusion. It's not humanly possible to stay in touch with that many people. The Bible tells us to be wary of having a multitude of unreliable companions, but to treasure those few close friends (Proverbs 18:24). Why? Because we are finite beings with a limited capacity; we cannot possibly keep up with as many people as we think we can. "The especially deep personal sharing and vulnerability . . . that we need . . . can only be achieved with a limited number of people. We haven't the emotional capacity to cope with any more than that."[6]

Just as it may be tempting to stay in touch with too many people, we may also be tempted to use the Internet as an unhealthy outlet. "For many, Facebook is less about looking up friends than it is about looking *at* friends."[7] I think too often we spend our days wasting time (that we really don't have) checking for updates on people we don't even really know or like. I don't mean to minimize the incredible benefits of modern technology, and I'm grateful for the ways I have been able to stay connected with friends online. Technology does foster true connection and relationship; however, we sometimes use media as an escape that keeps us from real, live community. Whether we use the Internet to zone out for a few minutes or to connect with a close friend, we need to examine why we're doing so and what it's accomplishing. Real community is going to cost us something. Are we settling for something predictable and easy as we log on and off at our convenience? Or are we taking risks that lead to rich community?

PRACTICE HOSPITALITY: WELCOME THE STRANGER

If we want to find friends, we need to make room for them in our lives; we need to practice hospitality. The word *hospitality* may conjure up images of cleaning or cooking dinner, and though that can be an important part of it, there's a depth to hospitality that goes beyond the literal welcoming of a guest into our house. In *Reaching Out*, Henri Nouwen defines hospitality as "the creation of a free space where the stranger can enter and become a friend instead of an enemy."[8] This inner hospitality requires the willingness to fashion a friendly, empty place in our heart—not just our home—for others to walk into. When we choose to be vulnerable with others and share what's really going on, it opens the door for them to step into our lives. When we focus less on how someone can meet our needs and more on how we can serve them, we make room for strangers to become friends. It's not easy to let people get close—to let them into our space (especially if we're not doing well, which may be the case right out of college). Sometimes we would prefer to remain strangers than to offer hospitality or seek it. But the Bible is clear that this is a serious obligation—that we must welcome the stranger.

Abraham modeled hospitality when he offered his finest food to three strangers who turned out to be angels come to tell Sarah she would have a son. Two disciples traveling on the road to Emmaus received a stranger, and when he broke bread they recognized him as

Christ.[9] It's our joyful duty to offer open, hospitable spaces where "strangers can cast off their strangeness," recognize each other as "fellow human beings" and become friends.[10] We never know who we may be entertaining or what the other person may have to offer. Abraham could have missed the opportunity to entertain angels, and had the two disciples ignored the stranger on the road, they would have missed Jesus!

There are many things that prevent us from truly creating space for people to move around in—even for ourselves to move around in! We don't know how to be poor in heart and spirit. We're so desperate to be filled—to have our desires satisfied—that we can't offer emptiness to others. We're so consumed with our own agendas, opinions, fears, jealousies and judgments that we make lousy hosts; there is little room for new friends, changed friends or old friends. As challenging as it may be, we must work to practice inner hospitality. We must work to welcome the stranger as well as to allow others to welcome us.

Alesha, a fifth-year senior, entered the year as an emotional wreck— the guy she'd been dating broke her heart, all of her close friends had graduated and, after two years of rooming with her best friends, she'd be living with all new roommates. With the exception of one, they were strangers. Alesha had a choice to make: retreat into her own pain and old patterns of not trusting other women, or welcome these strangers into her apartment and life. Alesha chose to practice hospitality.

For starters, she decided to be open and vulnerable about her own struggles. Rather than assuming these women had ulterior motives, Alesha assumed the best and let them break down her stereotypes (such as "women are always out to get me"). Her willingness to be real created space for them all to be real and vulnerable. Alesha also made a decision to make room in her schedule to be present with her roommates. Rather than comparing these women to the best friends of the previous year, she focused on ways she could serve and love her new roommates. This meant actually spending time at the apartment, choosing to do homework at the dining room table without ear buds and making impromptu meals together. In time, the dining room became a hub for conversation and connection as roommates passed through and sat down to talk or do their homework there as well.

The apartment wasn't perfect, and some of the girls made lifestyle choices that did not align with Alesha's values. But instead of getting upset with them, Alesha reached out. She remembers being frustrated with one of her roommates for repeatedly not cleaning up after herself, leaving dishes in the sink again as she sat in front of the TV to watch another show. Instead of railing at her for not holding up her end of the bargain, Alesha sat down next to her and asked if everything was okay. Her roommate burst into tears. She was not okay and needed a friend.

Practicing hospitality in the presence of these five women led to connections Alesha never expected. At the end of the year one roommate commented, "I'm going to miss you, and I'm especially going to miss your dining room table." Alesha's willingness to open her home and her heart allowed, in her words, "complete strangers to become best friends." If we want to grow in hospitality, we, like Alesha, can choose to

- assume the best or not make assumptions about others;
- be curious about others' lives;
- be open and vulnerable with our own struggles;
- enter new situations asking "How can I bless others?" versus "How can they fill me?";
- be interruptible, making room in our schedules and lives; and
- be physically and emotionally present.

SURRENDERING OUR PICTURE

If you would have told me that one of my closest friends after college would be a woman a decade older than me, I probably would not have believed you. But God was up to something.

My first apartment after graduation was a renovated farm house. Our landlord leased the top floor to me and my roommate, and as we hauled our belongings upstairs we noticed another tenant, Kathy, carrying boxes into the bottom floor. As we introduced ourselves and started to get to know each other, we sensed that she had a strong openness to faith—a journey that was just beginning for her. When we shared with her that we were looking for a church in the area, Kathy wanted to come with us. I'm nearly certain she would have tried any faith community, of any spiritual or religious affiliation, but God had a more specific plan. Over the next months and years she started seriously exploring Christianity. Today Kathy is still one of my closest friends, and because of what God was doing during those days when we were neighbors she is now my sister in Christ!

God used my roommate's and my willingness to love our neighbor and welcome the stranger to begin a work that makes a difference for all eternity. He also used Kathy in our lives to teach us many things about him and his Word, and to provide a soul friend in the next season of my life.

My story is similar to countless other alumni who opted to put aside their own vision to welcome new and diverse friendships into their lives. One recent alum, Martina, shares,

> One of my best friends from church is a nearly forty-year-old mother of five. She showed me what their family life was like, and let me come alongside them, both as a single and now married woman. I didn't think that I would find friendship in someone whose life was so drastically different than my own, but that's the power of the gospel—with Christ as our common denominator, other differences (like age and stage of life) become trivial.

If we think all of our friends have to be in the same life stage and share all of the same interests, then we are going to miss what God intends. He has something rich, deep and wonderful in store, but his plan may be entirely different from what we expect. When we surrender our picture, we open ourselves to endless possibilities and to the rich mosaic of God's best.

FINDING MENTORS AND DISCIPLES

As they pursue friendship postcollege, we encourage our recent graduates to look for three types of people: a Barnabas, a Paul and a Timothy.[11] The apostle Paul received encouragement from Barnabas (whose name means "son of encouragement"), and he discipled his protégé Timothy. In every phase of life we need people who will come alongside us and root for us; these Barnabas types can be peers or anyone who cheers us on, especially when we need it most. And we should be that Barnabas for others! We should also pursue a Paul—a mentor or discipler whom we respect. Finally, we should seek to train a Timothy—someone younger with whom we can share our lives as we follow Christ.

Though we may find a mentor at work or a Timothy in our neighborhood, likely the best hope for finding these relationships is within the local church. If we were mentored in college, we may be used to weekly sit-down meetings, but we might need to reframe our view. Many recent alumni meet with disappointment when they can't easily find someone to say yes to the "Will you mentor me?" question. Instead of asking someone to pour into us, we may need to look for people we respect and glean from their lives in other ways—perhaps while they're folding laundry, fixing dinner or working around their home. Similarly, as we invest in discipling others it may simply mean inviting someone to come alongside *us* as we do life.

SUMMARY

So how do we find friends after college? Be present, patient and purposeful. Practice hospitality and put aside your picture. Last, and certainly not least, plug into a local church (see the next chapter). Though there may be days after college when you long for the friendships you had during your undergraduate years, the transition will not last forever, and you will find new soul friends for the journey ahead. The company we keep has an immeasurable influence on the people we become. My prayer is that you connect with a community of believers—that you find a real place of belonging so that you can become all God desires for you to be.

GOING DEEPER

1. Who has come and gone on your friendship stage? How have you coped with the change?

2. What are your hopes and expectations for finding friends after college? In what ways may you need to alter your picture to stay open to change?

3. In what ways (attitude and actions) might you be tempted to settle for low-risk or false community after college? How will you avoid these pitfalls?

4. Can you think of a time when you were offered genuine hospitality? Describe.

5. How can you offer hospitality to others?

6. How will you plan to be a Barnabas, pursue a Paul and train a Timothy?

Scripture study: Proverbs 12:26; 18:24; 27:6; Ecclesiastes 4:12; John 15:13; 1 Thessalonians 2:8; James 2:23

Recommended reading:
Dietrich Bonhoeffer, *Life Together: A Discussion of Christian Fellowship* (New York: Harper & Row, 1954).

Jonathan Holmes, *The Company We Keep: In Search of Biblical Friendship* (Minneapolis: Cruciform Press, 2014).

Henri Nouwen, *Reaching Out: The Three Movements of the Spiritual Life* (New York: Image Books/Doubleday, 1975).

SIX

NO PERFECT CHURCH

CHOOSING COMMUNITY

You might see her actin' crazy
Be patient with her though cause she still God's baby
She the Church

LECRAE, "THE BRIDE"

WHEN SHAWN GRADUATED FROM COLLEGE he knew that finding a church should make his priority list, but it became more difficult in practice. Initially he moved back home with his parents, started attending their church and quickly concluded, "This sucks." The church lacked vibrancy, the preaching felt disconnected from his life and there wasn't a soul in his same life stage. Shawn hopped around to a few other churches but never plugged in. When he moved out on his own he chose an apartment in a rural area that offered affordable housing but not many church options. Feeling isolated and alone, Shawn poured himself into his work and then into a dating relationship with a woman who did not share his beliefs.

Shawn now admits that that his rural location and relationship distanced him from church for years, but he also didn't plug in because he "really didn't have a compelling reason." Regarding church he reflects, "I didn't know why I was there. A lot of people go for the social aspect and to reconnect with friends, but I'm an introvert. That wasn't a driving force for me. I guess I just always sort of struggled to figure out the why. . . . Why am I there? . . . What am I doing?" For Shawn, it became easier to listen to sermons on his way to and from work than to pursue the often exhausting experience of going to church. While the podcasts provided solid spiritual food and even sobered his mind enough to end his dating relationship, they were not a replacement for church involvement. It wasn't until he caved to a coworker's incessant invitation to check out his small group that Shawn finally found what he "didn't even know [he] needed."

After one visit Shawn joined his coworker's small group and his church—a commitment that came with a serious commute. Though the community had its "weirdness" and "wasn't perfect," it was incredible to be a part of "a group of twenty-somethings going after God." As Shawn reflects on this time, he talks about how central these people and church became to his living out his faith. His biggest regret is that he didn't say yes to his pestering coworker sooner. Looking back he feels like he wasted the first five years out of college. Because he didn't think he wanted or needed church, Shawn says, "I let every distracting thing I could find get in my way. . . . I think about how different my life would have been had I found that community sooner."

Without a convincing reason it's easy to question why finding a church matters. With so many virtual resources available, we may see church involvement as optional—nice but not necessary. In the challenges of transitional times, we may be tempted to forgo it because no one will know whether we go or not. It may feel tiring in the midst of other priorities or we may become frustrated when we can't find a church we like. As we begin to establish routines, it can be easy to leave church out—a decision that can dramatically affect our trajectory into early adulthood. None of us wants to find ourselves five years out of college with deep regrets about opting out. We need the church, and the church needs us. Church, in all of its mess and beauty, allows God to manifest his glory, us to experience community and the world to find hope. If we want to honor God and flourish after college, church matters.

WHY CHURCH?

If we're going to choose church, we need to know—deep down—*why* we go. Whether we go because we never thought not to, we struggle to show up or we have lost interest entirely, we need to be grounded in why it matters. Was church just some harebrained idea of a first-century moralist trying to keep society in line? Or is church Christ's plan to change the world?

In the Gospel accounts of Jesus, the word *church* (*ekklesia* in the original Greek) appears only twice, in Matthew 16 and Matthew 18.[1] In Matthew 16:13-20, Jesus discusses church with his disciples. After Peter confesses who Jesus is, "the Messiah, the Son of the living God," Jesus says that he will build his church upon Peter, the rock. Though Peter plays a foundational role, the stone is a greater metaphor pointing to Christ himself. Jesus wants his disciples to know that the church is built on him. What we believe about Jesus, who he is and what he did is the foundation for our understanding of church. Church starts with Jesus—the cornerstone and head.

If we want to keep Christ as the cornerstone, we must understand how he defines church. The term *ekklesia* literally means "called-out ones." Though it was used by governmental leaders in Jesus' day to refer to a gathering or assembly of people, when Christ envisions *ekklesia* it's something much deeper and grander than a political assembly. In contrast to the empire-building political movements of the day, Jesus calls his people to gather for a purpose that is not about gain or power, but rather about serving as a channel for his coming kingdom.

So what is church? Church is a body of believers called out for God's purpose. Church is not a building or an address, it's the *people* who come together to be on mission for God. Through this group of people Jesus plans to bring healing and hope to the world. Church is his primary strategy for bringing his kingdom, and when he returns in the end of time, he will return *for his church*, his bride.

So why do we go to church? If we're honest, many of us go to church because we hope it will help us change our behavior or do "me and God" better. Or maybe we like the praise band, the preacher or the feeling we get when we are there. Perhaps we go because we are hoping to meet a nice person to marry. Though none of these motivations is necessarily wrong, they should not be our primary driver in choosing church.

We should go because Jesus himself established *ekklesia*, and because we expect to encounter him there in the company of other believers. We go because Christ's church is *the* vehicle through which he plans to change the world. We go because we have been called out to come together, for our good and God's glory. Our going brings rootedness and accountability to our lives, and it honors God. We go to sing the songs and remind ourselves of what story we are part. When we come together we corporately declare what we believe and why we believe it. We go into our week with those reminders. If church is a gathering of God's people on mission, then we don't just *come* together, we *go* out from there to love the world.

GOING AFTER IT: IT'S UP TO US NOW

One of the biggest changes after college in our relationship to the church—as with every area of our lives—is that we have to be purposeful about choosing it. Perhaps like no other time, accountability structures have been removed and we must fully lead ourselves. For example, if we move to a new town and decide to sleep in each Sunday, likely no one is going to notice our absence.

When Clay graduated and moved to Atlanta, he researched church options online and took recommendations and contacts from his campus minister. Once he arrived, though, he learned that it was up to him to actually make those connections happen. Clay says,

> In school everything came at me as far as group meetings and opportunities. . . . Now, it's about searching things out, including church. Because there is such a diverse range of people and ages, you really have to seek things out. . . . The first three months out I was really in transition. I thought, "I don't know what I am doing!" I questioned, "Am I really supposed to be here, God?" I found my church about four months into moving, and that was big. A turning point, really.

Church provides stability in a chaotic time, but it's up to us to go after it. We need to decide whether being a part of church is something that's important to us. My hope and prayer is that you choose church. It's weird, messy and uncomfortable at times, but it is good. And it is an essential part of God's work in the world and our lives. When we say yes to church, we say yes to what God wants to do in us so he can do what he wants to do through us.

NO PERFECT CHURCH

Sometimes we don't choose church because we don't know how or we're not sure it matters. Other times we're looking for the perfect church, and when we can't find it, we give up and don't plug in at all. The truth: *there is no perfect church*. Church is made up of people. People are sinful and messed up, so churches are sinful and messed up. There's no real way around it; we are going to find something we don't like about every body of believers. Whether their musical style is not our preference or there are not many people in the same life stage as us or they serve bad coffee (out of Styrofoam cups!), we will inevitably find flaws with every church.

Sadly, I have watched alumni leave the local church because they were looking for the perfect church, and when they found that it didn't exist, they threw the baby out with the bathwater. Some walked away completely, some wandered for years and others "took a break" with the intention that they themselves would come up with a more Christ-centered expression of church. Sin has plagued the church for centuries, and we are not the solution. We are the problem, and the solution is Jesus himself. We must surrender our pride and choose to stand by the church, even in her flaws. Though we may want an exit ramp out, it's important to persevere in the midst of imperfections— for our sake, for the sake of others and for the future of church.

I have also watched alumni fail to plug in because they were looking for a church exactly like the one they were a part of in college or growing up, and nothing seemed to add up. *No two churches are exactly alike.* If you are looking for a church that is exactly like one from your past, you will be disappointed. Every church has its strengths and weaknesses, and this is the beauty of God's diverse body. We may find a church whose preacher is a less effective communicator, but perhaps the church's ability to show hospitality far surpasses our prior experience. We may find that the talent of the musical worship team is subpar, but perhaps this church makes prayer a priority not just in word but in action. It's okay to look for qualities that we appreciate, but we need to stay open to change.

As we do, hopefully we will experience the move of God in a new church and will be shaped in ways we never would have been in our former one. Though we often gravitate toward experiences that make us feel comfortable, sometimes churches that are distinctly different from our personal preferences offer opportunities for the most radical transformation.[2]

PLACE MATTERS: CONSIDERING MOVING
(OR STAYING) FOR A CHURCH

Some of our students meet with disappointment because they move to locations where Bible-believing, gospel-preaching churches are not readily available. There are geographical regions that offer a plethora of options, while others do not. This is important to keep in mind when contemplating a job offer or move. We encourage students to consider moving to a place where they know they will have church options, or if they're not sure what's next, we challenge them to move *for* a church community or church plant instead of for a job!

When Justin found out about a group of graduating peers and young pastors who were planting a church in Philadelphia, he thought, *What if I moved for the church and narrowed my job search?* Instead of moving for a job, as many do, Justin moved for Citylight, the church plant. In retrospect he's so grateful that he allowed the "where" (place) of his next step to be at the forefront of his decision making instead of the "what" (job). It's not that he didn't have any challenges his first year out, but he was able to commit to a place, mission and group of people that mattered. God provided not only a job in his field but a community in which he could flourish!

- -

Citylight started with seventeen people, half of whom were recent college graduates. Today Citylight is one church with two congregations, gathering around 450 every Sunday. Pastor Matt Cohen says, "There would be no Citylight without the alums who came to Philadelphia with us."

- -

DECIDE ON YOUR NONNEGOTIABLES,
BUT BE OPEN FROM THERE

There are a number of churches that do not look to Christ, teach heresy or fail to preach the gospel of Jesus. If Jesus is not the main event, if the Word of God is not accurately taught and if there is deviation from the true gospel of Christ, then this is a body to avoid. Here are some questions we should ask when looking for a local church:

- What do these people believe about Jesus? Do they confess Christ as Lord and Savior, and is he the cornerstone?

- Do they preach the full gospel of Jesus Christ, or a different gospel?

- Are these people on mission? Do they come together in order to *go* from there? (Or are they just an inward-facing holy huddle that resources its own self-interests?)

- Do they revere and teach the Word of God from Genesis to Revelation? Do they preach the authority of Scripture as God's revelation to us today?

- Does the congregation submit to the spiritual authority, care and discipline of the pastor and pastoral team?

- Is this church humble and teachable, willing to yield to the move of the Spirit and open to being wrong about something? Are they willing to embrace change?

- Is this a place where I can both grow and serve?

If our mindset is predominately consumerist, then we will shop for a church that makes us most comfortable. Or we will keep hopping around, switching churches when we find something we dislike or disagree with or when we feel that a church doesn't meet our needs. Though it's become hip to hop (especially in urban areas where there are many options), church hopping is not healthy for us or others. It keeps us from truly plugging in. To avoid this, it can be helpful to put a limit on the amount of time we spend looking (say three to four months). Once we find a church we can live with—it won't be ideal but may be exactly what God intends for our growth—we commit.

It's not wrong to desire to be a part of a church that meets our needs or feeds our soul. In fact, being a part of a body where we can be fed is very important. But we must also ask, How can I serve? and, How can my gifts be used for the good of others? If we can answer yes to the discernment questions above, then our concerns with the musical worship style or our frustration with the people who didn't say hi to us the first time suddenly become a little less major and more negotiable.

We need to major on the majors. We should have a list of a few (not fifty) nonnegotiable values that we are looking for, and then be open from there. We should also keep in mind first and second reasons for finding a church. When we focus on why church matters, we keep first things first and can put secondary needs or concerns on the back burner.

During college I had the opportunity to experience God in a variety of churches. Because of the time I spent in an urban area and abroad, I gained an appreciation for the unique ways in which God's people could come together. My church participation ran the gamut— from a small church that ministered to a number of homeless individuals in Philadelphia, to a high church experience in an Anglican church in Oxford, to a Brethren in Christ church in Harrisburg that was led by both a white male pastor and a Hispanic female pastor. These experiences grew my appreciation for the diversity of the body, but upon graduation—in my sin and pride—I became judgmental, thinking that because I had seen so much I surely knew exactly how church should be done. I had a long list of nonnegotiables, and I approached each new church with scrutiny, questioning whether it would ever measure up.

For example, from the first time I attended the church where I now worship, I quickly started checking boxes of things they did wrong in my opinion. The first Sunday I visited, two women cascaded down the aisles doing cartwheels and wearing T-shirts that read, "We Are Fun." This seemed flashy and irreverent. Their acrobatics were part of an announcement for a church picnic, and they pointed us to more information in the bulletin, printed on paper I thought cost too much with its glossy graphics. With my eyes focused on all of these externals, I wasn't looking for Jesus but rather auditing the worship service for flaws.

Then I joined the worship arts team. I met the ladies who did the cartwheels and designed the print resources. I got to know their motivations, and I realized that they had huge hearts for people who are far from God or who may never remember an upfront announcement unless it's showy. They made fools of themselves for Christ, for others to get connected. When I decided to get over myself, embrace serving and start understanding certain leadership decisions, I was schooled by a group of people with way more humble, gospel-centered hearts than my own. My initial nonnegotiables took a backseat as I started to put more meaningful things first. It's been over a decade since I showed up at that first arts meeting, and though I've seen my church at some of her most beautiful moments and some of her ugliest, I'm sticking by her, so grateful I didn't bail in those initial weeks.

PREPARING FOR THE MULTIGENERATIONAL ASPECT OF CHURCH

In our confidence and idealism, we may overlook one of the most important aspects of local church life: the opportunity to interact with people from other generations—children, teens, those in a different life stage and especially those who are older than we are. Unfortunately, many of us write off "old people." In a culture obsessed with new voices and fresh insight, it's hard for us to pause and appreciate our elders. I affirm the importance of hearing from upcoming, young leaders; however, will we spend as much time gleaning from those who have come before us?

Angela, a student who moved home one summer, questioned, "Has being in [a college town] spoiled me to only be comfortable with people my own age? Maybe I am spoiled. This past Sunday I was in an adult class [at church], and I was not happy about it. . . . I've been feeling like a square peg being jammed into a round hole within my home church community. I feel like I don't belong."

There will be times when we'll feel out of place. But it's important to be patient and open. *What can we learn from situations where most people are not in our life stage? What is God's invitation to us in this?* We need to prepare ourselves for the reality that life after college may involve significant interaction with people who are not in the same life stage—old, young and everything in between.

When Angela moved home after college, she made a choice to open herself to the older generation in her church. In this process she met with a delightful surprise: these seasoned, wiser individuals started calling out some of the God-given gifts inside of her, especially the gift of writing. As Angela was growing up on her parents' farm in a rural community, her family and friends had not necessarily encouraged her as an artist; her desire to write poetry had even been met with resistance. In contrast, these church members affirmed her passions. They also pushed her out of her comfort zone by encouraging her to serve both in and outside the church. Angela has volunteered as the editor of her church newsletter and currently helps with a mercy mission that gives away food and clothing to those in need. Opening herself to people not like her has led to deepening relationships, loving her neighbors and creating some beautiful writing!

WHAT IF I HAVE BEEN HURT BY THE CHURCH?

When my friend Rebecca was fifteen, she was sexually abused by a youth pastor who was twice her age. Eric played the part of the wise and winsome leader while preying on countless young girls. His actions came to light in the fall of Rebecca's senior year of high school when the sister of another victim exposed a sexually explicit text message. When confronted by the pastor, Eric apologized and made it seem like it was a misguided one-time error. He immediately asked Rebecca to delete his texts and keep quiet about the details of their relationship. She was "head-over-heels in love with him"; it never occurred to her teenage self that Eric was a sex offender. Eric was charismatic, charming and skilled at winning trust. So much so that when the other victim's family pressed charges, some members from the congregation sent out letters encouraging people to support Eric in court. Eric got off on the charge of "contributing to the delinquency of a minor"—the same hand slap that would be given to a college student who slips a beer to an underage drinker. He was asked to resign but was still given the chance to say goodbye at a send-off party with the youth group.

In the years that followed, Rebecca started to process what had happened. When another victim's mom sent her a copy of *The Wounded Heart*, she read it and wept. It was the first time she put words to the offense: sexual abuse. Rebecca sought counseling and began the long journey of healing. She started to see the ways the church had done such a poor job of protecting her and other youth. The incident had caused her to lose trust in men in the church and male leaders in general. Though she remained heavily involved in the church, almost as a coping mechanism, Rebecca suffered a world of hurt.

Sadly, issues of sexual abuse, extramarital affairs, verbally abusive leaders and mistreatment of members are all too common within the walls of many evangelical churches. When we have endured hurt caused by the church or by someone inside of it, we may feel our only option is to leave—not just a particular congregation but the church in general.

Rebecca chose a different path, but not just because she didn't know how to do otherwise. When she finally grasped what had happened, she said, "Thankfully my faith had grown so much through college ministry and small groups with peers, I was able to look at the church and say, 'No place on earth is an entirely safe place because it has sin inside of it.'" Part of Rebecca's healing involved her being able to separate Eric from the church. "Though the church didn't know how to handle the situation, and that's terrible, I tried to separate those two entities." She was able to forgive the church when she realized the members had been just as deceived by Eric as she had been.

Further healing came through an action the church took six years after the initial incident: they publically apologized, contacted the *Washington Post* to investigate and tell the story, and put policies in place to prevent something like this from ever occurring again.[3] Though some victims found the apology too little too late, Rebecca found the action incredibly helpful, especially in restoring her trust in men. She has since remained involved in a church wherever she has lived—while at college and in her post-grad location.

I in no way want to diminish the pain you may have experienced in the context of a church. At the same time, we must keep in mind that church is made up of broken, sinful people who hurt people. What gives hope is that we have a belief system like no other—one with the power and grace to find healing and forgiveness. As mentioned earlier, the only place besides Matthew 16 where Jesus uses the word *church* is Matthew 18. In this context he discusses a framework for forgiveness and reconciliation. The process is so central to church community that Jesus chooses to outline it for us. In what other belief system can we find the power to forgive and be forgiven? Our ability to pursue true reconciliation with the transformational power of the gospel sets us apart.

I have heard too many reasons why alumni no longer attend church. Some have been deeply hurt. Others are offended, frustrated or on their own vision quest to transcend the traditional practices that make up the church as we know it. Without realizing it, though, these individuals start to toss back and forth like infants in the waves (Ephesians 4:14). They lack the rootedness that comes with church connection, and they drift. Choosing church, even when we have been hurt, takes courage. It requires dying to ourselves. Being in community and accountable to one another is a discipline—for everyone involved. When we think we are exempt from these things, we hurt ourselves and others.

In severe instances, the most healing thing we can do is walk away and find a different congregation. Most of the time we opt to leave because we don't want to deal with stuff or to confront, forgive or live a certain way. However, there are occasions when leaving a church is necessary. Whenever possible, it is best to leave with the blessing of those in authority (a pastor or leadership team), but if this is not possible, we should find someone who can help. And we should not allow our experience with one congregation to keep us from life-giving relationships within another community.

Rebecca reflects, "I made an active choice in the course of my therapy while still involved in the church: I decided I was going to remain open to others even if that meant getting hurt. I realized that if I close myself off, I don't just keep myself from harm but also from the joy of being with others." Though Rebecca is more discerning than ever in her relationships, she continues to invest in the life of the local church—for God's glory and her joy.

PRACTICAL POINTS FOR FINDING A CHURCH

When it comes to finding a church after college, it's go time for our faith. We may find that our beliefs are put to the test as we question the wheres, hows and whys of getting involved. I urge you to ground yourself with good theology, ask the right questions, embrace proper expectations and go after it! Here are some practical points for finding a healthy body of believers:

- Don't assume that all regions offer gospel-centered churches. Consider moving (or staying) *for* a church.

- To locate a church, use your networks. Ask for recommendations from your current congregation, campus ministry or social media contacts. Word of mouth is a great resource.

- Research online. You can find out a lot about a church by perusing their website, reading their faith statement and listening to their sermons online.

- Find out about the church's mission and vision.

- Introduce yourself. Don't wait to be found.

- Attend introduction courses or congregational meetings.

- Meet with the pastor or someone on the staff.

- Ask about budget breakdown. What does this church care about?

- Find out about serving. Who in the church serves and where?

- Don't church hop for an extended time. Find one and commit.

GOING DEEPER

1. Why do you go/have you gone to church? What has been your primary motivation? Be as honest as possible.

2. How would you describe your ecclesiology (what you believe about church), and is there anything about it that you think needs to change?

3. You know yourself. What will it take for you to prioritize finding a church? What attitudes or actions can you put in place now for a successful transition into a church community?

4. What are some of your personal nonnegotiables when it comes to looking for a church? What will you put on the back burner as less important?

5. How have you dealt with conflict in the past? What can you learn from your previous experiences with conflict resolution that might be helpful in dealing with inevitable conflict in future situations?

6. What is one practical thing you can do today to help yourself or someone else find a church?

Scripture study: Matthew 16; 18; Acts 2:42; 5:42; Romans 12:4-5; 1 Corinthians 12:12; Hebrews 10:25

Recommended reading:

Gerald J. Mast, *Go to Church, Change the World: Christian Community as Calling* (Harrisonburg, VA: Herald Press, 2012).

Tony Payne, *How to Walk into Church* (Matthias Media, 2015).

Philip Yancey, *Church: Why Bother? My Personal Pilgrimage* (Grand Rapids: Zondervan, 1998).

SEVEN

PEOPLE ARE STRANGE

PREPARING FOR DIVERSITY

People are strange when you're a stranger.

THE DOORS, "PEOPLE ARE STRANGE"

IT "LOOKED GOOD ON PAPER" for Tyler to stay in the area of his alma mater. But despite having a job offer, a rich community and a local church he loved in the area, he took a leap of faith after graduation and moved to—of all places—Coatesville, Pennsylvania. Tyler moved to work with an organization called the Bridge Academy and Community Center (BACC), a faith-based organization that equips economically disadvantaged families and youth for success. Every day Tyler interacts with people who are very different from him and his background. The predominantly black and Hispanic population at the BACC contrasts with his upbringing "in a white family, white neighborhood, white school and then . . . predominantly white college." Tyler reflects on his education and experiences, saying,

"Though I had the chance to be around people from different backgrounds and races, I was still primarily around white people. Now, in my day-to-day meetings or when I'm with our students, I am sometimes the only white person in the room."

In order to be effective, Tyler's work requires him to have a range of diverse relationships. A typical day involves spending time with youth who have minimal parental support and zero financial means and who are in the middle of violence and school fights daily. At the same time, Tyler also interacts with upper-middle-class individuals when working with fund development or social gatherings. Tyler may leave a meeting with a potential donor, head to a meeting with a family in need and then engage a teen with issues related to school, fights or girls—each interaction drastically different from the next.

Tyler's job responsibilities stretch him, make him think differently and often force him out of his comfort zone. In talking about the tension he sometimes feels when trying to find common ground while also celebrating differences, Tyler says, "It's awkward, but that's okay." Despite the challenges, Tyler feels prepared to embrace the diversity he encounters. He loves the people he works with, and he loves his job. Because of the values instilled in him by his college ministry and mentors, Tyler has a huge heart for relating to people and situations different from him and his own experience; he's committed to "breaking down the awkwardness to get to the relationship."

Though your first job or postcollege location may not come with as much ethnic or socioeconomic diversity as Tyler's, there's a good chance you will experience diversity on other fronts. Whether it's moving to a large city or small town for the first time, interacting with people decades older in the workplace, joining a multigenerational church that approaches worship differently than you're used to, or engaging people with divergent worldviews, life after college is filled with opportunities to either welcome diversity or cluster in circles that feel comfortable and familiar.

Depending on your college experience, you may feel like your undergraduate years already exposed you to more diversity than ever before. If you're heading back home or staying in the area of your alma mater, you may find that it's easier to surround yourself with like-minded company than it is for alumni who move far away. Regardless, knowing how to welcome and interact with others whose backgrounds or ideas differ from ours is crucial for postcollege success in a diverse world. It's also essential to becoming more like Jesus—the One who welcomed every person, from every background.

FROM "BUBBLE" TO BIG WORLD

For most recent graduates, going from a college experience—where they are surrounded by individuals of the same age and life stage—to a postcollege setting where they may be in the minority of people like them comes as a culture shock of sorts. (Because of your upbringing or ethnic background, you may have been in the minority in many settings prior to this point; however, there likely will be an adjustment after college that will differ from your previous experience.) From the daily access we have to peers (through sheer proximity) to the endless opportunities to organize around personal interests (with student clubs and organizations), college is like no other time in that we can so easily and readily find people who are like us.

In some ways it may be hard to believe you will experience any culture shock or challenge adjusting to diversity. In an age of advanced technology, a global economy and rising international student enrollment, we are more connected to people and places that are different from us and our place of origin than ever before. However, we are arguably more disconnected and siloed. Because of the array of information and niche marketing, we can easily fill our lives (and our Facebook feed) with people and ideas that reinforce our likes, preferences and ideologies without really having to interact with different opinions. If we want to we can live in our own little bubble. On most campuses the structure of college life makes it even easier to do so.

As someone who attended a small liberal arts school, I can certainly say leaving college was like leaving a protective bubble. Even on a large campus, though, the bubble effect exists. At the large public university where I now work, the average student experience can still be very isolated. Like Russian nesting dolls, many students spend four years tucked inside the center of the state, inside the confines of our college town, inside the boundaries of the beautiful campus, inside the buildings of their major, inside the cocoon of their campus fellowship group. This is not to say that these students never venture from their "safe" place, but the nestled, homogenous experience of college stands in contrast to the people and place diversity they face postcollege. Whereas their friendship circles in college may have been dominated by relationships formed in their campus ministry, dorm, major or extracurriculars, after graduation they face a new social arena where a demographic of twenty-something peers with shared faith and an interest in ultimate Frisbee or ballroom dancing is not the norm. Making new friends, especially friends with shared interests, comes with significant challenge.

SO MUCH NEWNESS AT ONCE

For most, the undergraduate years serve as a prelude to full-on "real world" life (unless you attend a commuter campus or a community college where many people take classes while working or supporting a family). In contrast to previous adjustments, the change we undergo when leaving college is compounded because so many aspects of life shift at once. In prior times of change, there's a good chance that a number of things remained the same. Perhaps you spent a semester abroad in a previously unknown country, but while a part of your life changed, many aspects didn't: you still maintained your role as a student and a similar financial status, and maybe a familiar face from campus came along or you connected with other university-age students when you arrived. The transition from college to the next phase can be so overwhelming because it seems everything shifts simultaneously; it's almost too much newness to take in at one time.

In the book *Girl with a Pearl Earring*, the main character, Greit, reflects on a similar feeling of being overwhelmed with all the newness when she begins her first job as a servant in the home of the painter Vermeer:

> It was strange to meet so many new people and see so many new things in one morning, and to do so apart from all the familiar things that made up my life. Before, if I met someone, I was always surrounded by family and neighbors. If it went to a new place I was with [my brother] or my mother or father and I felt no threat. The new was woven in with the old, like the darning of a sock.[1]

Greit struggles to assimilate into her new setting because, unlike before, *nothing* feels familiar. She also shares how her brother experiences the same sentiments when he begins his first job: "[My brother] told me not long after he began his apprenticeship that he had almost run away, not from the hard work, but because he could not face the strangeness day after day."[2]

The strangeness of life after college can make us want to run from it all. We can feel lost, alone and unknown. You may have days when you are not sure you can face the strangeness all over again. And this may be the first time you have ever felt this way. You are not alone. Many alumni have gone before you, have shared in the same struggle and have lived to tell that this only lasted for a time until they established a new normal.

One alum, Tamara, shares her story about moving to a new city after graduation:

> Everything changed. New state, new job, new status as a working adult, new schedule with a different kind of free time, new

people, new church, new scenery, new living situation—everything. It lacked the familiarity of faces, friends, places, and namely, the comfortable.

In my first few months, I met the new with excitement. I discovered new favorite places on my own, I got to know co-workers, I introduced myself to strangers, I found new things to try. I filled my life to the brim with new, and ignored the feeling of loneliness that happened in the quiet hours when I realized I didn't have the support system I left. After a while, I just could not handle a life full of nothing familiar. And yet, I started to realize this was going to be my new normal. My reaction to this was to hold on more tightly to what I knew—friends, family, hobbies, faith.

This has all led to learning more about myself and my faith . . . that I can hold on to what I know, but not with a death grip. . . . [It's] taught me to ask myself questions—to take a step back to understand more of my purpose, so that I can enjoy and embrace what God has provided. It's been a transition—an ongoing, changing one—but a transition that I'm starting to enjoy and get excited about.

Although the transition into all the newness can make us want to retreat to what's familiar or judge what we don't understand, there's great hope. The God of the universe has gone before us in the newness. He is the one who goes ahead of us to level the barriers and roadblocks in our path (Isaiah 45:2). Nothing is too weird or strange for him. In fact, everything, including diversity, was his idea.

DIVERSE BY DESIGN

From Genesis to Revelation, the Bible is the story of a God who values and designs diversity. From Babel (Genesis 11) to the Great Commission (Matthew 28) to Pentecost (Acts 2) to the great multitude of every tribe, tongue and nation worshiping together (Revelation 7), we know God intends diversity. When the kingdom comes in fullness, people from *all* nations will unite together under one banner. This unity doesn't mean uniformity, but rather a beautiful picture of hearts joined together in love for God and one another while we simultaneously maintain those distinctives that make us unique.

The future picture of the coming kingdom in all of its diversity has implications for today. As Christ-followers we have the responsibility to embrace people who are different from us. As tempting and comfortable as it may be to surround ourselves with people who are similar to us, this is not God's intent. Though it's crucial to have like-minded friends for the journey ahead, it does not mean we hang out solely with people who are exactly like us. By design, God desires for us to interact with people who are dissimilar because those interactions shape and change us, hopefully into people who model more of Christ's character. In fact, God may place us in a situation after college where we are forced to befriend people who are the last ones we'd handpick as our primary community.

A couple of years out of college my friend Lauren and I decided to lead a Bible study for other young women. Mostly we were just looking for an excuse to gather some of our favorite people together on a weekly basis to study God's Word and encourage each other. We sat down and made a list of about a dozen women we wanted to join us. We prayed, picked our study material and passed out invites. Our handpicked small group started coming together—with one glitch. The women we invited also knew other women. The word spread, and people started coming out of the woodwork, cold calling us to see if they could be a part. This was not our plan! We wanted to hang out with our friends, not a bunch of random women.

Lauren and I had a choice to make: stay selfish or split up and lead two different groups on different nights in order to welcome as many women as possible. In the end, we got over ourselves and decided to offer two studies. Though I probably would not have handpicked this unlikely group of women (and I'm guessing many of them felt the same about me), God used that small group to refine each of us in ways we could not have imagined.

When we realize that God has placed us in the company of people who are different from us (whether in our church, job or neighborhood) because he wants to use those people to refine us, we can have a better perspective when we rub each other the wrong way. There's a good chance that friction whittles away pieces of us that are not pleasing to God or teaches us something about ourselves that we need to work on or confess (such as pride, jealousy, greed or selfishness). Perhaps it simply brings a new perspective that we need now—or for the future.

LESS LIKE US, MORE LIKE CHRIST

When we make our focus less about finding people like us and more about being like Jesus, we open ourselves to an incredible journey. Embracing diversity and getting out of our comfort zone is good for us, is good for others and brings God glory. The Scriptures are filled with stories of God's people and what happens as they embrace new and different experiences, sometimes willingly and sometimes not. Abraham left Harran, Moses led an exodus from Egypt, Daniel pursued faithfulness while exiled in Babylon and Jonah finally went to the uncomfortable land of Nineveh. Jesus spoke to the Samaritan *woman*, turning things downside up ("For Jews do not associate with Samaritans," John 4:9). Paul entered the marketplace at Athens to engage the thinkers and philosophers of the day. As these people left their comfort zones and aligned with God's plan, they served as a signpost, pointing people to him.

When Jessica Jackley shares her story, she starts by remembering a moment when she realized her life had become too comfortable. In fact, she "started to do funny little experiments to shake things up."[3] She spent a semester at sea in the Shipboard program, traveling to new countries and continents. She shaved her head. After college she moved to California, where she engaged new ideas that challenged her thoughts about the global poor. This led her to quit her job, move to East Africa and listen to the stories of people there. All of these experiences—far from her comfort zone—undoubtedly laid the groundwork for an incredible contribution as cofounder of Kiva. This microfinance organization has loaned millions of dollars to help the global poor become entrepreneurs in the world.

When we let go of what's comfortable, we invite God to transform us and others. Though our choice to move to an unfamiliar place or engage someone with a different perspective may not lead to the start of the next million-dollar microfinance organization, it can allow us to "become less" and Christ to "become greater" (John 3:30).

BE THE ONE WHO WELCOMES: DECIDE IT'S NOT ABOUT YOU

As important as it is to welcome and expect diversity, there's a deeper commitment we make when we proactively decide to be the one to make someone else feel welcome, even when we personally are not all that comfortable yet. It's easy to default to a mindset that expects others to go out of their way for us. In many ways the college experience reinforces this attitude. From the design of the dorm, to the drink selection in the dining hall, to the paved paths across campus, college is set up for you. Not long ago Penn State launched a marketing campaign that branded university life with the line "It's *Your* Time." Implicit in this slogan is the idea that college is about you. The classes, professors, programs and extracurriculars are all for *you*. Though maybe not intended, the problem with this tagline is that it reduces college to a consumeristic carnival ride of sorts (with everyone working harder to make sure students have a good time), rather than celebrating the ways college can and should train students to serve others, the community and the world—during their time as students and afterward with their degrees.

You will likely learn quickly that life after college is not about you. Nothing is set up for you or your postgraduate peers. Though this can come with confusion and frustration, it also creates an opportunity to live out Jesus' call for us to die to self and serve others. When we decide that we will be the one to welcome someone else, we make a commitment to forgo our own need for comfort in order to serve someone else.

Myra, a self-described introvert, has modeled this in her new work environment. Not only has she faced diversity when asked to manage a project that required overseeing employees who are decades older than she is, but she also chose to go out of her way to reach out to another coworker who seemed to be having a hard time finding friends. Because he didn't participate in certain social outings with his coworkers (like weekend drinking parties), he took heat for it. Myra, still trying to find her own footing, invited him to connect with some of the twenty-somethings she's been getting to know at her local church. Her coworker accepted her invitation and has even started coming to church regularly. When we decide it's not about us, God uses us to bless others. The reward: we are blessed in the process.

PRACTICAL KNOWLEDGE AND POSTURES FOR WELCOMING DIVERSITY

As we prepare for the diversity we will experience postcollege, there are some basic values and postures that can equip us to engage. Though Tyler admits that "there has definitely been a learning curve in faithfully loving people," he also says that he's "figuring out how to ask, listen, and be honest." Here are some other practices that help him—and others—embrace diversity.

Leave your comfort zone. When we leave what seems safe to experience something new, we decide it's not about us—a first step in welcoming others. It's important to go to people and spend time with them in places that matter to them rather than waiting for them to come to us. Learning and understanding happens in the context of relationship. We need face-to-face time with others, on their turf. Leaving our comfort zone may mean going to a new place or country, or it could simply mean walking across the room to introduce ourselves to someone new. It could mean trying a new food, going to an event with someone even if it's not something we'd normally choose or offering to watch someone's kids. If we want to welcome people who are not like us, we need to leave our familiar and safe spots and learn about someone else's.

Listen. In many ways listening has become a lost art. Even when we're in a conversation, we're often distracted, waiting to make our point or thinking about something else. Or we're watching our cell phone that we've set on the table before us, a gesture that tells the other person that we're anticipating something more interesting or important. If we want to listen, we need to be present. We need to get off the screen and make eye contact. We need to ask good questions and genuinely care about the other person's response. True listening occurs not just when we understand someone but when the other person knows we understand—when they feel heard and think, *You get me.* Even if we profoundly disagree, we can still listen well. When is the last time you truly felt listened to? What did the other person do that made you feel that way?

Research shows that "when two people are talking, the mere presence of a cell phone on a table between them or in the periphery of their vision changes both what they talk about and the degree of connection they feel."[4]

Offer empathy. In a famous line in Harper Lee's *To Kill a Mockingbird*, Atticus Finch says, "You never really understand a person until you consider things from his point of view. . . . Until you climb into his skin and walk around in it."[5] If we want to offer empathy, we need to place ourselves in someone else's shoes and experience their world from their point of view. As we interact with people who are different from us, let's do our best to understand their story or the battle they're fighting. Tyler says, "Being a white guy in a predominantly black city working with a group of black and Hispanic women and children has given me insights that most are not privy to." He's garnered these insights because he's taken the time to step into other peoples' world and see things from their viewpoint.

No action or exchange should be stripped of its humanity, but we do it all the time. We can become easily frustrated or combative with someone without realizing that they are created in God's image. The telemarketer, the disgruntled boss or the hostile employee is still a person with their own story and struggles. When we put ourselves in the skin of that mean coworker and realize she's a single mom with three young kids, working full-time and usually sleep deprived, we can cut her some slack and love her better. Maybe even offer to make her a meal or slip her a gift card so she can take a night off from cooking.

--- --- --- --- --- --- --- --- --- --- --- --- --- --- --- --- --- --- ---

A compilation of seventy-two studies over thirty years shows a 40 percent decline in empathy among college students, with most of the decline taking place after the year 2000, coinciding with the rise of cell phones and other technology.[6]

--- --- --- --- --- --- --- --- --- --- --- --- --- --- --- --- --- --- ---

Practice civility. What would our conversations, our nation, our world or our government look like if we truly listened to others' opinions without hostility, disagreed without disrespecting and balanced our deepest convictions with true open-mindedness to hearing someone else? In a culture where we're so quick to combat, destroy and disrespect, the practice of civility—"claiming and caring for one's identity, needs and beliefs without degrading someone else's in the process"—has become another lost value.[7]

Not long ago two senators, a Republican and a Democrat, were willingly marooned on an island for a week. They "wanted to demonstrate that a Republican senator and a Democratic senator could survive together on a deserted island without retreating to separate red and blue lagoons."[8] Acknowledging the lack of trust across party lines, they aimed to model the bipartisan relationship building they wanted to see throughout the Senate. Believing that trust comes from knowing the "other," the two men offered a simple proposal to their peers: monthly lunch dates with senators from the opposite party (like those held decades ago). They believed a cure to the brokenness in Congress starts with communication and trust across party lines, and they wanted to be part of the solution.

From this example on a national level we learn that we can work closely with others even when we have wildly opposing views. As Philip Yancey writes, "The issue is not whether I agree with someone but rather how I treat someone with whom I profoundly disagree."[9] How do you approach conversations with people who hold different values and views? Do you aim to win an argument or do you seek to understand?

Don't make assumptions. When we choose mutual respect, it means we refrain from making assumptions. We look for common ground first rather than differences. Instead of interpreting peoples' actions through the lens of our stereotypes, we clear the slate of our preconceptions and assume the best. How would our conversations, interactions and communities change if people treated one another with mutual respect? How might our world be different if we actually listened to and learned from each other rather than made assumptions?

One college senior, Pearl, asked, "*How* do you connect with people different from you?" We start by deciding that it matters. In the same way the apostle Paul encourages us to "clothe [our]selves with the Lord Jesus Christ" (Romans 13:14), we need to put on postures that allow us to embrace others. Stepping into a posture is not something we do half-heartedly. When we decide to dress ourselves with the posture of mutual respect, civility, empathy, listening or learning, it affects our whole person and demeanor. It communicates to others that we genuinely want to know them and understand them. With these in place, connecting with people who are different from us can be as simple as our approach to any other relationship. Because, in fact, we are all different from each other, and yet we are all the same in that we are made in the image of God. We need the right heart and spirit, but we don't need to overcomplicate it. Just be yourself and let the other person do the same.

Life will be filled with opportunities to either welcome, seek out or avoid interactions with people who differ from us—in opinion, politics, upbringing, education, age, lifestyle choices, economic status, ethnicity and worldview. If we want to be effective and engaged Christ-followers, we need to faithfully embrace diversity, even though it may be strange and stretching. As we opt in, let's prepare ourselves for the reality that it may change us—hopefully in ways we never imagined possible.

GOING DEEPER

1. Discuss your college experience. What opportunities have you had to interact with people who are different from you? In what ways have you surrounded yourself with people like you?

2. How can you prepare for diversity? As you think through your new (or upcoming) circumstances, consider five "unlikely" people you may meet. What are some practical ways in which you could serve them, get to know them or learn from them?

3. When was the last time you did something outside your comfort zone? What did you do and how did it affect you or others?

4. Consider the five practices for welcoming diversity. Which is easiest for you? Most difficult? Why?

5. How can you use technology in a way that fosters genuine connection rather than reducing it? Do you have any ground rules when it comes to your cell phone or media usage (such as putting the phone away during mealtimes or meetings)?

6. What's one thing you can continue, start or stop doing to become more effective in relating to people who are different from you?

Scripture study: Matthew 28; John 3:30; Acts 2; Romans 13:14; 1 Corinthians 12:13; Ephesians 2:19-22; Revelation 7

Recommended reading:

Patty Lane, *A Beginner's Guide to Crossing Cultures: Making Friends in a Multicultural World* (Downers Grove, IL: InterVarsity Press, 2002).

Richard J. Mouw, *Uncommon Decency: Christian Civility in an Uncivil World*, rev. ed. (Downers Grove, IL: InterVarsity Press, 2010).

Randy Woodley, *Living in Color: Embracing God's Passion for Ethnic Diversity* (Downers Grove, IL: InterVarsity Press, 2001).

EIGHT

FAMILY MATTERS

RELATING TO PARENTS

*At some point you pardon the people in your family for
being stuck together in all their weirdness, and when
you can do that, you can learn to pardon anyone.*

ANNE LAMOTT, *TRAVELING MERCIES*

"HEY, ERICA, HAVE YOU SEEN MY TATTOO?!" Connor called to me across a crowded room, lifted his T-shirt and revealed huge letters that arched across his back: INHERITOR. When I asked what made him choose this word, Connor said his decision was "semi-spur-of-the-moment," but after we talked I learned that it was far from thoughtless. The tattoo is about identity—about being a child of God, an *inheritor* of the kingdom. Having grown up in a "messed-up" family and in a culture that feeds us lies about who we are, Connor said, "I wanted a permanent, lasting reminder of who I am in Christ." The tattoo influences the way he views his family and every other relationship. He is *not* an inheritor of a broken family legacy or of lies about his identity. Though Connor has experienced feelings of

isolation and abandonment from his family, he knows he's never forsaken by God. He is an inheritor of the greatest treasure: the riches of heaven and adoption into Christ's family forever.

If you were raised by humans, you likely agree that families are messed up. Even the most loving parents have not raised their children perfectly, and the family you grew up in is no exception. My pastor's wife, one of the most amazing parents I know, jokes that instead of putting money in a college fund for her children she's saving for their future counseling sessions. She knows that her kids will inevitably have issues to deal with because of her parenting. When it comes to family life we will all have stuff we need to work through, and our upbringing will undoubtedly impact our relationship with our parents as we transition out of college and build future relationships.

FAMILY OF ORIGIN, FAMILY OF GOD AND FUTURE RELATIONSHIPS

Our family of origin is one of the most significant factors in shaping us into the people we are today. Our upbringing—for good or ill—influences the way we approach life: how we relate to our parents and other family members; how we handle conflict; how we view money, work, sex and so on. The perspectives and patterns we adopt affect the way we will interact with a future spouse and how we will raise our own families if we get married and have children. That said, our families do not ultimately define us. Yes, they have influenced us (hopefully in some incredibly positive ways), but we are defined by a greater reality: Jesus Christ. He can transform, undo, heal and restore all of the brokenness that comes from growing up in an imperfect family. He alone defines us.

As Christians we have been adopted into a new family, and our identity is son or daughter of the living God and loving Father—even before we are a [your surname]. Because of Christ, we can look at our current family situation through the lens of the gospel. We give thanks for all of the positive things we have gained from growing up in our family of origin, and we trust God for the redemption of the places that are messed up right now. Whether it's dealing with your parents' recent divorce, a strained relationship with one parent, a struggle to meet your parents' expectations, a complicated sibling situation, the tension that comes from living with parents after graduation, or communication challenges, there are countless dynamics involved in relating to parents and family, especially in this next phase of life.

Some recent graduates are particularly aware of how broken their families are, while others are in denial about growing up in an imperfect family. The twenties are the years to deal with family stuff. Yes, we will have family dynamics to deal with throughout our lives, but there may be no greater opportunity than the "defining decade" of our twenties to establish healthy habits with our parents.[1] The relationship between you and your parents is transitioning, and it should be.[2] You should be moving from dependence to more independence, which should ultimately lead to a healthy interdependent relationship as an adult (you) relating to adults (your parents). As you transition out of college, both you and your parents have adjustments to make, in expectations and also practically. Be patient with the transition, and begin to ask questions such as:

- What do I want the relationship to look like?

- How do I maintain the good aspects of our relationship?

- How can I improve the relationship?

When it comes to relationships with family, we need to understand where we have come from (past issues and patterns) and where we are going (God's vision for our future and hope for what the relationship ought to be). We need to acknowledge that our families are not perfect, but God is not finished with the work he wants to do.

Note: If your parents have passed away or you do not have a current relationship with them, the content of this chapter can apply to relationships with guardians or other authority figures in your life.

FORGIVE YOUR PARENTS, HEAL YOURSELF

Forgive Your Parents, Heal Yourself is the title of a well-known book by a Jewish psychiatrist, but it might as well be the mantra for many twenty-somethings. Whether your family issues are in the forefront or you have never really thought about it, these years are a great time to reflect on your upbringing and invite God to transform places that need his touch. This doesn't mean you have to go romping around in all of the mud puddles of your past or that you need to see a therapist. However, if the Holy Spirit reveals something you need to work through, there's nothing shameful about seeking out a trusted mentor or counselor.

Inevitably there's something about our upbringing that we wish we could change—choices our parents made in raising us; how they treated each other; how they handled adversity, discipline, money or living out their faith (or not). And if we're honest with ourselves, there's something we could have done differently as their son or daughter. This is where forgiveness comes in. When we choose to forgive our parents or other family members, we let go of our past as well as our hopes that our childhood could have gone differently. We release ourselves to heal. Anne Lamott says,

> I tell you, families are definitely the training ground for forgiveness. At some point you pardon the people in your family for being stuck together in all their weirdness, and when you can do that, you can learn to pardon anyone. Even yourself, eventually. It's like learning to drive an old car with a tricky transmission: if you can master shifting gears on that, you can learn to drive anything.[3]

In her first year out of college, Jada faced one of the most difficult decisions of her adult life: forgiving her father. She and her fiancé were nine months out from their wedding date when their premarital counselor asked them to write letters to their parents to honor and thank them. From a divorced home, Jada could easily write to her mom, but she had nothing to say to her dad. While she was growing up he was emotionally distant and verbally abusive. He forced her to earn his love through achievement, approving when she excelled and cutting her down when she failed. He lectured instead of listened, always talking about the news or politics and never asking about how she was doing. He treated her mother and other family members with the same abuse—patterns he learned from his own upbringing. Though Jada wanted to write something, she could only think about the hurt he had caused. She stared at a blank screen and cried.

Then Jada called out to God for words and just began typing. As she clicked away, she sensed God pulling out positive memories from the past, reframing stories where she had seen only the negative. Scene after scene from her childhood crossed her mind, but the pictures looked different than she once remembered. She began to better understand her dad's intentions in certain situations. She even looked back with compassion on some of his decisions. Jada started to see her father through God's eyes. Though she cannot forget the pain of her past, something broke that day. Jada chose to let go, to forgive.

Writing that letter was a "defining moment," and it has forever changed Jada's relationship with her dad. She reflects, "Forgiveness was so freeing. . . . I didn't pigeonhole him in this place anymore, and our relationship has gotten better and better over the years." As Jada chooses to view her father through a new lens, she talks about the importance of "standing on that first forgiveness." A lifetime of unhealthy patterns does not disappear in an instant; Jada's father has done and said many hurtful things since the day. As she "practice[s] that forgiveness going forward," Jada is so grateful for that initial letter—a tangible reminder of her *ongoing* process.

Learning to forgive is one of the hardest, best and most important things we can do in this life. And it's central to the gospel Jesus came to show us. As Christians we are part of a story that's all about forgiveness. The moment we forget this, we get tight-fisted—the opposite of the open-handed life we're called to lead. Forgiveness is a choice, not a feeling. Our decision to forgive is crucial for our healthiness and for faithful Christian living. As we choose to forgive our parents or family members for their offenses, we can also resolve to not make the same mistakes in raising our own family. We forgive and live into a new legacy, making change for generations to come.

Note: in certain circumstances, the healthiest position may involve not having a close relationship with your parents or one parent in particular. Healthy boundaries may be necessary (at least for a time), especially in situations of abuse, neglect or abandonment or if a parent struggles with addiction or mental illness. Only you and God know the healthiest plan for relating to your parents. For the purposes of this chapter, however, we are going to assume that you are working toward a relationship with your parents (or guardian). We also hold out hope for any relationship, no matter how damaged. The God of the universe can heal and restore even the darkest, most broken places.

SHOULD I HONOR MY PARENTS OR HONOR GOD?

When we ask, "Should I honor my parents or honor God?" we often want to know which is more important, and we unfairly pit one against the other. These directives are not necessarily mutually exclusive. My pastor describes these two commands as opposite banks of the same river.[4] As we journey down this river, we acknowledge that part of honoring God means honoring our parents. In Exodus 20:12, God says, "Honor your father and your mother, so that you may live long in the land the Lord your God is giving you." We are called to honor and respect our parents no matter what age we are or what life stage we are in. We do this by showing them that we value them and by acknowledging that they are still our parents even though we now take personal responsibility for our lives.

One way to honor your parents is to put yourself in their shoes. They are going through their own transition as you go through yours. They may be grieving as you graduate, leave your growing-up home and pull away from them. If you lived with them during college or plan to stay under their roof, be mindful that a transition still can and should take place. Even if we have a strained relationship with our parents, we can try to view things from their vantage point. Or better, we can ask God to help us see them the way he does. When we commit to praying for our parents—who are individuals with their own needs, struggles and hopes—our empathy and compassion grow. Likely they did and are doing their best to raise us given how they were raised. As we think about their story we can come to love, honor and respect them even more—even if they are not Christian believers.

Respecting our parents doesn't mean we grant their every wish. We can respectfully disagree with them while still having honor in our hearts for them. There may be times when our parents want us to do something that we know will not honor God. Though we are called to respect our parents, Jesus says, "Anyone who loves their father or mother more than me is not worthy of me; anyone who loves their son or daughter more than me is not worthy of me" (Matthew 10:37). This statement is part of a discussion with his disciples about the cost of following him. We are called to honor, obey and follow Christ above all else.

Sara, an alum who has great respect for her parents, shares a story about almost losing her relationship with them over a disagreement about her decision to go to Indonesia for a midterm missions trip. Feeling "caught in between what I clearly felt God guiding me toward and my parents' wishes," Sara struggled to know what to do.

> I felt so torn. I knew that it was important to honor our parents; however I knew it was more important to honor God. I knew that this was what God was leading me to. I also knew enough to know that the presence of strife didn't mean that I was out of

God's will. I pressed into him and moved forward, feeling the intense pain of a broken relationship with my mother. God was so good to me though, and I found reassurance in him.

Departure day came and my parents decided that they wanted to take me to the airport, surprising me. As it was time for me to get to my gate my mother hugged me and with tears in her eyes told me that she loved me. When I returned she would tell me that she was just so scared for me and was so sorry. She was proud of me and my choice to do what I knew was right and honoring to God despite resistance.

Our loyalty to God's call may mean we disappoint our parents. We should do all we can to respect them (and hopefully most of our decisions allow us to honor God and our parents at the same time), but we also must obey God above all, even in the face of adversity.

Though our parents have undoubtedly made mistakes, we can also try to see what they've done right. We can honor them by thanking them for the positive principles they've instilled and healthy decisions they've made. We can give them feedback on how what they've taught us is helping us now (in areas such as work, finances, relationships and faith). Telling your parents how their investment is bearing fruit in your life may be the single most meaningful, encouraging and relationship-building thing you can offer.

On a family vacation one year, my sister and I took the opportunity to thank our mom for sacrifices she made as a working mother when we were young—a decision that we all reflect on with mixed emotions. The chaotic time of my early twenties brought some of the dark side of that decision to the surface, forcing me to deal with issues that stemmed from having a mom who—for many years—worked long hours with a rough commute. Over the last decade or so, we both have been able to process how her absence affected our relationship. We've had tough conversations and named hurtful places, and we continue to learn how to love each other better. While it has been hard and messy at times, this heart work has paved the way for the life-giving relationship we treasure now.

I know that my mom looks back on my childhood with significant regret for not being there more, but I wanted her to know that while her choice had hurtful outcomes, much good has come from it too. Because she wasn't hovering over us at every turn, my sister and I learned how to solve our own problems and make decisions. Her model as a strong female in the workforce empowers us to lead with wisdom and strength in our own careers. The risk she took as the first in her family to pursue a college education inspires us with a legacy we want to share with our own daughters. And her willingness to help us work through our own mixed emotions as we balance work and motherhood has been invaluable. As my sister and I help our mom reframe some of the past, it has an incredible impact on our relationship today.

FROM DEPENDENCE TO INDEPENDENCE TO HEALTHY INTERDEPENDENCE

As we embrace adulthood and begin to take full responsibility for our lives, we will likely face challenges that tempt us to call on our parents to rescue us. As my husband, Craig, and I currently raise young children, we constantly ask them (especially when it comes to potty training!), "Do you need my help, or can you do it by yourself?" Unless we are severely ill or injured, it would be silly for us to imagine our parent helping us go to the bathroom as an adult, but sometimes we still ask for help in childish ways. As we launch into life after college, our goal should be to move from dependence to greater independence and responsibility. Perhaps a good question to ask is *Do I need their help, or can I do this by myself?* More and more we should be able to answer, *Yes, I can do this.*

This doesn't necessarily mean that we interact with our parents less or that we no longer seek their wisdom and counsel, but it may mean changes in *how* we interact. For example, one alum, Ryan, describes the shift in his relationship with his parents in terms of going from "child" to "peer." He says, "My parents are some of my biggest mentors, but I have stopped seeking their permission for every decision I make. Now, I'm able to reasonably, honestly push back on decisions they want me to make." At times he simply informs them of certain decisions rather than asking for their feedback.

Here are some practical steps for moving from dependence to healthy interdependence:

- Avoid codependence. If you rely solely on your parents (or they rely solely on you) to meet social, emotional, spiritual or financial needs, it will be important to break away and establish healthy boundaries. When one recent alum realized she and her mother were codependent, she started by simply contacting her less frequently. It was strange at first (and even more confusing for her mother), but she gradually began to gain confidence, make decisions on her own and report outcomes after the fact. Another alum with a codependent parent realized that "I can't take care of my mom; I need to take care of myself." If he opts to visit home, he limits the time to two days.

- Get family-related loans paid off efficiently. The financial tie can sometimes keep other aspects of the new relational context from maturing.

- Ask for your parents' input (where appropriate) about major decisions. This will communicate respect and serve to mature the connection between two adults.

- Report successes that you have when they occur.

- If you want to be treated as an adult, it's important to function as one. This may mean avoiding financial dependence, offering to help or serve your parents, or taking responsibility for your actions.

- If you move home after graduation, have an open discussion with your parents before (or shortly after) coming back. Talk about their expectations for you while you are living under their roof. Also, be upfront about your intentions on how long you plan to stay. Showing them that you're acting like a respectable adult will hopefully motivate them to treat you as one.

You may find that though you are working toward healthy habits, your parents are not. In a situation like this you need to keep in mind that we cannot control other people, but we can own our part. Some parents (without even realizing it) may try to use you to get their needs met or manipulate and control you because of their own unhealthiness. These actions may undermine the healthy steps you are trying to take. Do your best to fight for a positive relationship, but understand that you cannot change your parents. Jesus can. We each need to decide what is healthy for us and stick to it. And it's crucial that we continue to take responsibility for our part.

CHOOSING HEALTHY COMMUNICATION

Current technology allows us to communicate with friends and family members at the click of a keyboard or touch of a phone screen. Though we may have unlimited access to our family, we need to decide what type of communication is the most productive and healthy. I've mentored recent graduates who struggle with basic decision making because they rely too heavily on their parents for advice, contacting them multiple times a day; they needed to figure out how to establish new ways of relating in order to become emotionally healthy and independent. While we can be too attached, it's also possible to swing in the other direction, without even realizing it. As we desire autonomy, we may need to be mindful to not get so busy that we neglect to keep in touch. There's not necessarily a right or wrong when it comes to the frequency or form of communication we use, but our motivations (*why* am I contacting my parents [or not] right now?) and the outcomes of our actions (is this accomplishing something positive and healthy?) do make a difference.

As you establish yourself in your postcollege context, consider how your communication with your parents may or may not be fostering a healthy transition. If you tend toward constant contact with your parents and they are some of your only confidants, you may be missing an opportunity to deepen relationships with people in your current community. Or if you're inclined to distance yourself, you may ask, How is my communication (or lack thereof) cultivating the relationship I want with my parents?

LIVING WITH YOUR PARENTS AFTER COLLEGE

More and more recent graduates are moving back in with their parents. Regardless of your reasons for heading home, be prepared that it can be overwhelming for everyone involved, especially after you haven't lived there for a number of years. It will be important to anticipate potential tension, work to actively manage it, articulate expectations and (in most cases) move toward finding your own living situation. At the same time, moving back home could be the best opportunity to grow and strengthen your relationship with your parents.

In 2015, 26 percent of young adults were living in their parents' homes, up from 22 percent in 2007. The percent of college graduates living with family has increased despite years of economic recovery.[5]

During his senior year Jordan was not looking forward to living at home, but he wasn't sure he had another option. It wasn't until he heard a positive story from a friend who had moved back home for a short time that he started to think, "This doesn't have to be a bad thing." Because of his major (film studies/production), Jordan needed access to career opportunities in areas where housing was often not affordable. Moving back to his parents' home in New Jersey positioned him to search for jobs in Philadelphia and New York without sinking financially. Jordan says, "Living at home has provided me with the flexibility to take financial risks I couldn't have afforded to take had I been living on my own." More than that, his relationship with his parents has grown.

> Moving back home after college has allowed me to continue to spend time with them, get wise advice from them and be a source of joy for them. When I was in college, I thought I was supposed to interact with my parents less and less, so I could mature and become independent. But now I see that I still need their wisdom and perspective, built on years of experience I don't have yet. Living with them has taken away the need for an excuse to call. They're there. When I have a question, I can just ask.

Though the move back home has not been without challenges, overall Jordan and his parents have strengthened their relationship through this experience. Jordan has saved money after securing a job with a production company he loves, and he plans to launch out on his own soon, grateful for the foundation built over the past year.

As you navigate family life after college, keep in mind that it may get messy at times, but we serve a God who delights to roll up his sleeves, stoop down and make things great (Psalm 18). Family stuff can be weird, tiring, frustrating and confusing, but it's too important to ignore. Family matters, and the potential for what God can do in and through you and your family is huge—in this next phase of life and for generations to come. Pray and trust God to work. Invite him to move you and your family members toward God-honoring, appropriate relationships between mutually respected and loved adults.

GOING DEEPER

1. What do you appreciate most about your relationship with your parents? What would you change?

2. How can you show honor and respect to your parents right now? What are some things your parents have done well or right in raising you?

3. Is there a family member you need to forgive? How can you take a step toward that forgiveness?

4. In what ways are you moving from dependence to independence? What do you need to start, stop or continue doing in order to move toward a healthy interdependent relationship with your parents?

5. Describe your communication with your parents. What motivates it, and do you think your current patterns are fostering healthy habits? Why or why not?

6. What is your greatest hope for your family and future relationships with your family members? How can you live, act and pray toward that hope?

Scripture study: Exodus 20:12; Psalm 18; Matthew 10:37; 18:21-22

Recommended reading:

Henry Cloud and John Townsend, *Boundaries: When to Say Yes, When to Say No—to Take Control of Your Life* (Grand Rapids: Zondervan, 1992).

Leslie Leyland Fields and Jill Hubbard, *Forgiving Our Fathers and Mothers: Finding Freedom from Hurt and Hate* (Nashville: Thomas Nelson, 2014).

NINE

TWENTY-SOMETHING RELATIONSHIPS

NAVIGATING SEX, DATING AND MARRIAGE

Your twenties matter. Eighty percent of life's most
defining moments take place by age thirty-five.

MEG JAY, *THE DEFINING DECADE*

"I SLEPT WITH SOMEONE AGAIN," Hayden confessed to her mentor. This time it was a man from her Alcoholics Anonymous meeting.

With a compassionate tone, Maria challenged, "Hayden, you don't want to be forty years old, still figuring this stuff out." Hayden paused. It was the first time she really thought about the future impact of her current sexual decisions.

Hayden started drinking and sleeping around her freshman year of college. She grew up in the church, but once she started partying and hooking up, she felt judged, especially by "virgins who didn't struggle in the same way." She tried attending a campus fellowship group but "never felt good enough" for it. When she confessed her struggle to one of the leaders, she simply counseled Hayden to stop her behavior. The leader told her to say no but never gave her something to say yes to. Hayden reflects, "She didn't give me something to live *for*. . . . I didn't know *how* to stop." Drinking helped her feel less socially awkward, and sex made her feel wanted. Throughout college, Hayden slipped in and out of sexual relationships while also ducking in and out of her fellowship group.

After graduation, Hayden moved to a new location where she knew no one. She started drinking with coworkers and turned to the bar scene for one-night stands. She had reached a new low of drinking alone, and her sexual behavior became riskier than ever. In a sober moment, Hayden realized that her lifestyle choices were not working. The stakes felt higher now that she had a job to hold down.

Unsure where to turn, Hayden reached out to a leader from her former fellowship group. This leader passed her the name of someone in her new location who led a Bible study for young professional women. Maria welcomed Hayden with grace and took the time to get to know her. She encouraged her to see a therapist and attend AA.

The day Hayden shared about her AA hookup, Maria told her, "You can choose behaviors that are healthy, but they hurt more because they form different grooves in your brain." That conversation was a turning point. Hayden did not want to waste the next two decades trying to "figure it out." She desired to be in a healthy relationship and married someday. From that day Hayden resolved to change. That was the last time she's slept with someone.

The topics of sex, dating and marriage carry great weight in themselves, and while transitional times offer an opportunity to start anew, they also bring increased challenges and temptations. No matter what our sexual history, struggles or desires, the chaotic time of life after college can make things even more confusing. Often our familiar supports are gone, we're still establishing ourselves in a community and we're feeling lonely.

We may struggle with the following:

- looking for stability in an unhealthy relationship
- compromising our standards because we lack accountability
- questioning our values when we're in a setting with different expectations
- hooking up with a former boy/girlfriend because we long for intimacy
- finding comfort and control in sexual addiction, pornography or masturbation
- becoming consumed with finding a mate
- becoming consumed with career or fear of commitment
- wanting to end our marriage because it's harder than we envisioned
- feelings of same-sex attraction, sexual identity confusion or knowing how to respond to our LGBT friends[1]

No matter what our struggles, fears, hopes or hang-ups, it's important to prepare for potential obstacles as well as glorious possibilities! We need to know that our twenties matter. Our attitudes and actions in these years shape who we become when we're forty.[2] And we don't want to wait until then to figure this stuff out! Whether we're dating, married, wanting to date and marry, or we don't desire it right now, this next decade is not a holding pattern—these are years to be *lived* faithfully, regardless of our status or struggles. If we're going to navigate these complex issues with real faith, we need to debunk some myths, then look at how we pursue healthy patterns and pathways.

MYTH 1: ONCE WE FIND OUR PERSON, OUR LIVES BECOME STABLE

When everything around us is changing it's normal to desire stability. People are one of God's greatest gifts to us in any life season, but it can be challenging to know how to approach relationships when we're in transition. Whether we just got married, we're currently dating or we're hoping to find someone, we may be tempted to look solely to that relationship (rather than the Source of that gift) for constancy. Or, if we're single, we may be tempted to compromise our values when faced with increased pressures, loneliness or a new environment with different influences. I know alumni who were committed to saving sex for marriage and kept those boundaries while dating in college, but when they moved away from their friend group and mentors they struggled and started having sex. I know others who've slept with an ex or with a former friend because they were hanging out and "one thing led to another." Other recent graduates enter unhealthy relationships, especially when looking for "that person" to offer constancy in a dynamic time.

As a college student, Clark lived a "sold-out" life for Jesus. He dated here and there, and despite chances to compromise his physical boundaries Clark pursued purity. After college, he moved five hundred miles from his alma mater and closest friends. Though lonely, Clark felt excited about the journey ahead, including the possibility of meeting a life partner. He held his standards close: "Only date someone long-term if she has the same beliefs and an active Christian faith." At the same time, Clark started to see every new person as "an opportunity to just see what was going on."

When Lia, a woman from work, invited him to grab dinner one night, it seemed harmless since he knew nothing about her. As they hung out, they learned they were similar in countless ways—not only in their professional interests, but also their love for sports, taste in music and sense of humor. By the third date, Clark realized that he "really liked Lia, but she didn't match with [his] values." He knew he needed to break it off, but the fact that he saw her every day and people at work were excited for them made it complicated. Though they had made out a few times, Clark decided to end the physical part of the relationship and remain friends. As they continued to hang out, however, Lia kept pushing for more physically.

One night they went "way too far." They slept in the same bed, and though they didn't have intercourse they crossed more boundaries than ever before. The next day, Clark knew he had compromised, but he was really attached. Lia had become a companion. Despite these feelings, Clark found the courage to break it off completely—a move that hurt both of them immensely in the short term, but something Clark knew he needed to do to honor God, his convictions and Lia.

Clark says, "It was a chaotic time, and I thought if I could have one thing settled . . . if I had 'my person' in the midst of it . . . I could find stability." He confesses, "I compromised in the chaos of the transition and in the absence of community. . . . There was no one to hold me accountable." Feeling the normal tension of any twenty-something with a sex drive combined with pressure from coworkers and his deep desire to find a partner, Clark made a mistake he hopes other recent graduates avoid.

Dating Lia did not bring stability. In fact, it created more confusion for both of them until Clark broke it off. Since then Clark has made a commitment to have the "faith conversation" from the get-go. Though it can be awkward, it's a crucial filter. After a number of nos following his relationship with Lia, Clark eventually met a woman through online dating who made her convictions clear in the first line of her profile: she told viewers to read no further if they didn't share her faith in God. So far things are going well, especially since they have a common language to talk about dating and boundaries!

Though the temptation to search for our source of stability in a relationship may seem like a caution for singles, it can also apply to those who are in a committed dating relationship or marriage. Karissa, who got married right after college, shares, "When everything seemed to be changing I knew Tim was a constant, but I wish I would have known God would use Tim's imperfection to teach me to lean more on *him* and not depend solely on the man who was so seemingly perfect when I decided to marry him." God uses people—including the most intimate human relationship of a marriage partner—to bring comfort and companionship, but our ultimate stability and security come from him alone.

MYTH 2: THE WINDOW FOR MEETING OUR MATE CLOSES AFTER COLLEGE

Many recent alumni express concerns that if they did not meet their potential mate in college, they missed their window. Though there are few experiences where we are surrounded by so many individuals in the same life stage, *we did not miss our window.* Right after college I attended more weddings than I could count. Many of my college friends met their spouses in college, and my single friends and I celebrated these joyful unions (trying not to feel sorry for ourselves). This past summer, my husband and I were invited to *eight* weddings—and only one was for a recent graduate couple. The rest were friends who met their mates after college; for some, *years* later. If you didn't date in college, you're not behind the curve, and if you haven't met your mate, the door to that possibility is far from shut.

If we're single and desire a relationship, it's important to not see our status as a holding pattern until we get to that next thing. We need to embrace the potential of our life stage *now.* Last time I checked, Jesus himself led the ultimate life as a single! The apostle Paul encourages singleness because it allows for "undivided devotion to the Lord" and the Lord's concerns (1 Corinthians 7:32-35). Singleness opens us to do anything, go anywhere and serve the kingdom in ways that are unique to our status. These years offer opportunities to serve overseas, travel, volunteer and savor our alone time with Jesus.

Social and mass media often glamorize dating and family life. When we fill our views with snippets from Facebook, TV or movies, we can convince ourselves that our lives don't match up. One single confessed, "I just took Instagram off my phone." It was hard for Megan to see married people, families and even other singles portraying their "picture perfect" lives because it made her feel like she needed to do the same. Instead of comparing her life to an image feed on her phone, Megan is choosing to *live* the life God has provided.

It's not always easy, and there are days she feels incredibly lonely even in her church community, but Megan continually reminds herself that she does not need to "cloak [herself] in shame because [she's] single." God loves her just as much as a single as he would if she were a wife. When Megan reflects on the beautiful web of relationships God has provided, she says, "These [friendships] are not my consolation prize. They *are* the abundant life I'm living here and now."

While single we can choose to put ourselves in places where we can meet people. One alum, Danae, says that she's not looking for marriage right now, but she also doesn't want to "corner myself in a small cluster of non-Christian, non-datable guys." She wants to get to know a number of men, even if she's not ready for marriage. For Danae, meeting people outside of a few men from work and church means involving herself in hobbies and allowing her friends to introduce her to others. Since she doesn't feel "wired for online dating," Danae takes advantage of the connections she already has. She allows her friends both near and far to "advocate" for her, introducing her to others at social events or setting her up on blind dates.

If we're single, it's important to evaluate why we do or do not want to be married. We may desire or delay marriage for the wrong reasons. Too often we idealize marriage. We expect too much from it, believing it should bring ultimate personal happiness. On the other hand we may be cynical; we have no hope for our own marriage as we have watched our parents' or others' marriages fail. We may be too afraid or too selfish to give up our freedom for the hard work of a marriage relationship.[3] Whether we're idealistic, pessimistic or both, we need to assess our views, search our motivations and ground ourselves in a healthy understanding of the purpose of marriage. If we're obsessing about it, let's make sure our ideal is something that exists. We may need to spend time with married couples we respect in order to create a more realistic picture. If we're keeping marriage at arms' length, we need to be mindful that marriage isn't just a button we press when we're ready. If we casually date for a decade or sink years into a relationship that's not going anywhere, we don't get this time back. How can we, like Danae, stay open even if we're not ready now but desire marriage someday?

For those who are married, how can we advocate for single friends? Will we open our homes and lives instead of only hanging out with other married people?

MYTH 3: COHABITATION IS THE MOST PRACTICAL SOLUTION

"We're planning to live together when we move to Chicago," Ava told me. She and her boyfriend, Jason, had been dating for most of college. She was headed to graduate school, and he planned to find a job. Financially it seemed most feasible for them to move in together.

Ava and I starting meeting at the beginning of her senior year to study the Bible, something she had never really done before. As we built trust, Ava confessed that she and Jason had a sexual relationship, but she felt convicted that it didn't honor God. When she and Jason talked about it, they agreed they needed to make a change and abstain. As their relationship and spiritual lives grew healthier, their decision to live together before marriage seemed like a step backward to me. I asked Ava how they had concluded that cohabitation was the best option. She told me that this was a way to save money while she was a student and they prepared for a wedding someday. From everything I knew about Ava and Jason, I believed they were pursuing Christ and loved and respected each other. I challenged her: What if you got married *before* you moved?

While the vast majority of unmarried young adults
want to be married at some point (82%), it's not
a priority right now for most of them. And, in fact,
they'd like to get a lot of things in order first.[4]

At first this seemed preposterous. How could they possibly plan a wedding in just a few months? But as she and Jason discussed it, the idea of having an intimate ceremony where they could join their lives in the presence of God and a few others before moving in together seemed to make sense—both biblically and practically. They got married in July and moved to Chicago as husband and wife the following month.

When we think we need a year to plan the perfect wedding, we may conclude that living together first makes sense, but we may overlook the *most* practical solution: get married. Though marriage is not something we should enter lightly or because we need a practical fix to a problem, we should evaluate ways in which our culture has influenced us to elevate the wedding day to an ungodly height. It's an amazing day, but it's just one day. We should also be mindful of the way more and more people view marriage as a capstone—something to do after we have all our ducks in row—rather than a cornerstone—a foundation to build our adult lives on.[5]

Americans are getting married later and later. The
average age of first marriage in the United
States is 27 for women and 29 for men.[6]

If we feel we need to get our lives in order first, we may miss out on some of the incredible benefits of marrying young. According to newlywed Tim, the advantages include "companionship, starting a

home together, sex, and always having someone who has your back."
For his wife, Karissa, "marrying young means that we get to build our
lives together ... to be a critical part of shaping the person you're going
to spend the rest of your life with." When we invest in a person when
we're young, we spend less time stacking up "things to bring into a
marriage" and more time figuring out how to live our difficult, ordinary lives together.[7] Karissa says,

> Marriage opened up a whole new chapter of growth: personally,
> relationally and spiritually. When we make marriage out to be
> for people who are "grown up," it makes it seem like you get
> married and everything is happily ever after. Tim and I do not
> have it all together. Our fights and struggles are very real, but
> through [it], we learn in a more profound way what real love and
> acceptance is.

If we unnecessarily delay marriage, we may be tempted to pursue
unhealthy, low-commitment encounters or even cohabitate with
someone who does not end up becoming our life partner. I know
alumni who moved in with their boy/girlfriend because it seemed
like the most practical solution at the time. Unfortunately some of
them (especially women) waited for a marriage proposal that never
came, while others ended up heartbroken after *years* of investing in
the relationship.

Not only is the choice to live together before marriage misaligned
with God's purposes, but there are also research studies that link cohabitation with higher divorce rates. The "cohabitation effect" can
cause people to "slide" into marriage; they may end up marrying
someone they shouldn't because it's easier than breaking up. Also,
there's a "sunk cost" when the relationship doesn't end in marriage.
"Each additional investment into the relationship makes it that much
harder to end [it]," and the time spent with that person could have
been spent meeting someone more suited.[8]

> *"Two thirds of Americans will cohabitate with a relationship partner, and one half of marriages emerge from cohabitation. . . . Research has shown . . . premarital cohabitation actually appears to lead to higher divorce rates in many Western countries."*[9]

MYTH 4: WHAT WE DO IN THE BEDROOM
IS NONE OF YOUR BUSINESS

Our culture has made sex public but not personal or communal. In *Real Sex*, Lauren Winner talks about how sex is public in the sense that people disclose intimate details on talk shows and expose their bodies or make out in plain view. But we have no common language to talk about the impact of our sexual decisions on others. We're not supposed to talk honestly with others because it's no one else's business. Even if we don't agree with what the Bible teaches about sex, the idea that sex only affects the two consenting people is a lie.[10]

Though we may be culturally conditioned to see our sex lives as individualistic, the reality is that sex forms us, and our choices affect others. We should care when someone has an affair or premarital sex or decides to cohabitate. And we should allow others to care about us. If we want to pursue faithfulness, we need to let others in to "our business." This doesn't mean we hang our dirty laundry or share with everyone, or that we become voyeurs, gossips or people who judge others. It means finding a few trusted friends or mentors we're willing to let in. It also means being willing to have hard but grace-filled conversations with friends who have let us in.

When Craig and I were dating we made a commitment to save sex for marriage, but without the help of the Holy Spirit and the community around us I'm not sure we would have made it to the wedding night. We both had people in our lives who knew our boundaries and asked us hard questions. We also had a married couple who met with us and guided us into important conversations about communication, expectations and sex. When we got engaged, they encouraged us to consider a short engagement.

Despite my hesitations, Craig convinced me that four months was plenty of time to plan a wedding. He said, "We have an incredible community who will help make this happen." He was right. I will always look back on that perfect day and see the patchwork of people who made it possible—Esli ironing tablecloths that morning, Barb pulling an all-nighter to print programs, Mel flying in from Texas with elaborate items to decorate porta-potties! Our family members and friends made more sacrifices than we know (and we're so glad they're still our friends after it all!). More importantly, it was and still is our community that helped us pursue faithfulness to God's best while dating and now in marriage.

If we want our sex, dating and married lives to honor God, we need to submit ourselves to a community that will help us, and we need to *be* that community for others. When Hayden started to find healing from her sexual addiction, Maria and the Bible study women provided a grace-filled space. Hayden reflects, "I needed community. It was the first time I felt like I could be myself without being judged. At first it was super awkward . . . I felt a lot of shame. But it was that group that held me accountable." Maria showed her that she was valued no matter what, and she gave her something to live for: God's design for relationships.

Men who struggle with looking at pornography report that building honest friendships with other Christian brothers decreases temptation and leads to more victory over their struggle.[11]

GOD'S DESIGN AND DESIRE

Simply put, God designed sex for marriage. Every other expression is out of sync with God's best for us. Because our culture has normalized a way of living that God never intended, this truth may be difficult to swallow. As Christians we are called to live in a way that does not make sense unless we know God. Choosing to follow God in this area of our lives will set us apart, no doubt. But with the Holy Spirit and help from other Christians who truly care, we *can* fully live in the ways God has designed for us.

God made us sexual beings, and God made sex—a good and beautiful gift. However, God's intent for the *expression of sex* is inside the covenantal commitment of a marriage between a man and woman. Why? Because there is no other context that sanctifies what actually takes place when two people come together sexually. God says *no* to sex outside of marriage because his *yes* to sex within marriage is so necessary.[12] He desires to protect and care for us by having us reserve this gift for someone who says yes to us forever, and who loves us for far more than what we can offer sexually.

Premarital sex (intercourse or oral sex) is not a handshake—it's a sin that takes its toll. When we give and take what's meant to be given away in marriage, we rob what was meant for someone's future spouse, and we undermine God's purposes for our bodies and lives. Our sin never affects us alone. It always affects other people. For example, do you want to tell (or hear from your future mate) stories about prior sexual encounters? A pornography addiction? The person you (or they) previously lived with? Talking with a potential future spouse about your past sin or theirs may be one of the most painful conversations you'll have, but you can make decisions now to change or to not create a past that you'll regret.

HOW DO WE RELATE AND DATE IN A WAY THAT HONORS GOD?

Some have argued that our culture is "post-dating," replacing all the traditional dating rules and rituals with "hooking up" or "hanging out."[13]

More than ever, we need ways of interacting with the opposite sex that help us discern whether a relationship could lead to dating and marriage. Though relating to the opposite sex is more of an art than a science, we can think in terms of five levels.[14] They are not a checklist or rigid grid but more like benchmarks, where one level progresses into the next. These levels can help us define where we are in any relationship:

- respect
- admiration
- interest
- affection
- love

All relationships must begin with *respect*. Showing respect means that we will not mistreat, intentionally hurt or mentally undress the other person. We are called to respect all individuals because they are God's children; however, we do not need to respect every person's decisions, behavior or character. If we're getting to know someone and find out that they behave in a way we do not respect, we should not date them. We must respect the person we marry.

At the *admiration* level, we begin to notice qualities in the other person that we admire. These may be character traits such as courage, honesty or responsibility. Though we can have a number of individuals that we admire but will never date (friends, coworkers, family), it's crucial to admire the person you intend to date or marry. You may even make a list of some key qualities you hope to see in a future spouse.

Admiration moves to the *interest* level when we discern we want to get to know this person better. We see potential because we respect and admire them. This level can be a bit awkward, especially when we're not sure whether they have interest. You or the other person may even be interested in more than one person at the same time. Therefore it's important to be clear with your intentions in this stage.

The interest level moves to *affection* when we continue to spend more time with the person, there's a spark and we want to be around them almost all of the time. We begin to see this person as someone we could potentially spend the rest of our lives with and we want to be with them exclusively. Unfortunately, most relationships start in the affection level and have to work backward from there. We may find ourselves fooling around with someone physically, only to realize we don't really respect them or we see character issues. At this level it's key to have healthy boundaries in your relationships (discussed more below) and to acknowledge that you are probably more "in like" with this person than "in love."

Love completes the levels. Though love involves affection, admiration and emotion, it is also a choice and commitment. Love is the level where you declare to each other, "Forsaking all others, I do." Love is not a throw-away word; it communicates devoted attention to the relationship that is different from all the other levels. When my colleague Johnny was dating his now wife, Kathy, he vowed not to use the *love* word unless it was followed by "Will you marry me?" He knew its weightiness. In fact, Scripture uses marital love as a metaphor for Jesus' love for the church—a love that literally lays down its life in an act of pure selflessness (Ephesians 5:22-33; Philippians 2). Love is serious, selfless and sacrificial. It lasts through different seasons and storms of life, and it goes far beyond affection. Physical intimacy bonds us with another, and sometimes when we share that we stir up love before it's time (Song of Songs 2:7). We may think we love a person, but love is deeper than the feelings we get and bond that forms from having gone far physically.

We need to ask what we're willing to give away (physically, emotionally, spiritually) to another person at each level. Our hearts, minds, souls and bodies are treasures that we should not just throw before anyone at any level. Let's respect ourselves and the other person enough to be wise about what we share and how much.

HOW DO I FIND "THE ONE"?

A Christian professor who taught my freshman Bible 101 course claimed that any man and woman who are Bible-believing Christians could be matched for marriage and it would work. I was appalled by his suggestion. I protested with the passion of someone who believes in *romance, soulmates* and *love!*

A decade later I got married myself, and after being married for some time, I don't think my professor was as absurd as he came across to my freshman self. Though there's something to be said for marrying a person you connect with, the fairytale I had in my head back then is far from reality. Love is a choice, not a feeling. Craig still takes my breath away, but most moments of our marriage are built on choices, commitment and service to each other in the ordinariness of life (laundry, dishes, diapers).

One of my former neighbors, Riya, and her husband have an arranged marriage. Over tea one day, she shared with me that she received criticism from Americans who could not believe she gave herself to a man someone else selected for her. In response, she confessed that she could not comprehend how we Americans keep giving ourselves to people sexually without any commitment. The day Riya married, she joined with a man who said *yes* to her alone, forever.

If we truly want a biblical view on dating, it would actually come a lot closer to Riya's story. The Bible is full of arranged marriages. Though we do not have such a practice in our culture, one principle to take away is that dating and marriage may be less about finding our soulmate and more about committing to a partner we *choose* to love and respect. We may feel a deep connection with someone who is not a believer or a healthy partner. The spark is important, but it's not the only thing that makes a marriage last. Similar to finding a church, we don't want to land somewhere unhealthy, but we also need to know there is no perfect one out there—and we're not perfect either. Choose wisely, and choose to commit. Once we marry, that person *is* "the one."[15]

Here are some questions to consider if you are contemplating marriage:

- Do we share active Christian faith and commitment to following Christ?
- Does this person draw out the best in me, push me closer to Christ and care about my growth?
- Do I see God at work in and through this person?
- Do I respect, admire and trust him or her?
- Can I fully be myself when I am with this person?
- Do we have strong communication, especially in times of conflict?
- Do we have similar dreams, goals and desires in life?
- Do we share a sense of humor?
- Do our close friends and spiritual mentors support the relationship or do they have concerns?
- Is God speaking to me about the relationship, and am I being obedient to what I hear?

HEALTHY BOUNDARIES IN DATING

When we start dating someone, we have no idea whether that person will become our spouse. We should treat this person as God's child and someone else's future spouse. In the chance that it doesn't lead to marriage, we want to know that we did "good, not harm" to them and to their future spouse (Proverbs 31:12)—and to our future spouse and ourselves! Most importantly, we should keep each other pure because we want to pursue holiness and honor God with our bodies.

Though I cannot tell you the exact boundaries you should have in your dating relationship, I strongly encourage you to consider what God would desire for your good (and your partner's) as you keep the big picture in mind. Craig and I kept similar boundaries to ones Mindy Meier shares in *Sex and Dating*:

- Don't sleep overnight in the same bed.
- Keep clothing on.
- Don't touch body parts that are covered by a two-piece swimsuit for women or swim trunks for men.
- Don't lie on top of each other.[16]

You may opt for different boundaries than these, but the most important thing is that you seek God, you have boundaries and you know why you have them. Regardless of the details, these principles can apply to all:

- Establish your boundaries before you start dating.
- You may date someone who has different boundaries than you. Don't compromise for fear of losing the relationship. If someone respects you for more than what you can offer physically, they can respect your boundaries.
- Let your care for the person motivate you to pursue purity instead of stirring them up sexually.
- You cannot do it alone. Find an older, wiser person who will ask you the hard questions.
- Have grace with each other. If one or both of you violates a boundary you set, talk candidly about what needs to change, and then together commit to the new limitation.

We need to keep our eyes and expectations in check. Our partner cannot meet the needs and longings only God can. If we're looking to a relationship for security or significance, then we may need to move in a different direction or we may need to ask God to refine our heart when it comes to relationships.

As you navigate the challenges and opportunities related to sex, dating and marriage, commit to these things:

- Trust in God's character.
- Ground yourself in a godly view of singleness and marriage.

- Spend time with both single and married people you respect.

- Pursue purity and prayer. Be discerning about the media you expose yourself to.

- Invest in and initiate connections within a healthy community of believers.

GOING DEEPER

1. What are your biggest hopes or fears when it comes to dating and marriage?

2. What myths are you most tempted to believe and why? How can you walk in God's truth instead?

3. What stood out to you about the five levels of relationships? What can you apply to a current or future dating relationship?

4. What other questions would you add to the "questions to consider if you are contemplating marriage" list?

5. Have you thought and prayed about your physical boundaries in dating? If so, what has God revealed to you? If not, why?

6. Are there current attitudes or actions that you need to change when it comes to sex, dating and marriage? If so, what next step can you take today?

Scripture study: Song of Songs 2:7; 3:5; 8:4; 1 Corinthians 6–7; 13; Ephesians 5; Philippians 2

Recommended reading:

Timothy Keller, *The Meaning of Marriage: Facing the Complexities of Commitment with the Wisdom of God*. New York: Dutton, 2011.

Mindy Meier, *Sex and Dating: Questions You Wish You Had Answers To*. Downers Grove, IL: InterVarsity Press, 2007.

Lauren Winner, *Real Sex: The Naked Truth About Chastity*. Grand Rapids: Brazos, 2005.

PART THREE

REAL WORLD

FAITHFUL TO OUR CALLING

TEN

ON PURPOSE

STEWARDING EVERY AREA OF
OUR LIVES FOR KINGDOM GOOD

Earth's crammed with heaven,
And every common bush afire with God.

ELIZABETH BARRETT BROWNING,
"AURORA LEIGH"

"I FEEL LIKE I'M AT THE FINISH LINE WITH NOWHERE TO GO," Deisha admitted to me in April of her senior year. After months of applying to jobs, she had yet to receive an offer. "What am I supposed to do with my life?" she wanted to know.

Not long after my conversation with Deisha, I talked to Faith. Three years after graduation, she was struggling with job dissatisfaction. After a "soul-draining" internship entering data for a local business, a stint in college ministry and a shelf-stocking job at a public library, she confessed that she thought she would have found a stronger fit by that point. She compared herself to peers who graduated at the same time. They all seemed to have found their "callings" while she remained stagnant and confused.

The question, What should I do with my life? is a normal one to ask during our senior year and our mid-twenties—in fact, it's one we might continue to ask throughout our lives. Searching for job fit as well as discerning our calling is a lifelong, life-wide process. As we grow and change professionally (as does the job market and our employers), we reevaluate and recalibrate. It's normal to change jobs or even careers multiple times over a lifetime.

Not only does our calling evolve as we better understand ourselves professionally, but it also deepens when we connect it to every area of our lives. When we talk about what we should be doing, often we think only in terms of a job, but vocation is "never the same word as occupation, just as calling is never the same word as career."[1] If we want to be faithful to all of the "callings" God has on our lives, we should always be asking what he wants us to do. Our answer directly affects how we fill our days, how we respond to our world. If we're questioning our calling, we need to get beyond just what we'll do for paid work, important as that is. Our calling is deep, wide and multifaceted.

WHAT IS CALLING?

I don't really like the word *calling*. It's not the actual word that bothers me but rather the confusion it often carries. The mainstream has hijacked it and made it simply about finding our career. Monster Jobs tells us "your calling is calling," Oprah wants to help us find what we're meant to be doing and Forbes offers twenty "how-to" tips.[2] The culture has also robbed calling of any sense of a Caller—the voice of the one doing the calling.

But it's not just the mainstream that muddies calling. I think the church has also added to our heap of confusion. Too often the church makes calling about discerning our one true passion as if it's "a gold nugget buried within the river bank."[3] If only we could search more diligently, dive deeper, we'll discover it. Often this diving involves looking inward to see how God has uniquely made *me*. Though I do believe God has deposited talents and passions within us, often we make calling too much about us—about what we should be doing for God (or for ourselves) instead of about responding to what God has done and is continually doing in the world.

If we're unsure about what we should be doing or if we don't feel a "sense of calling," we may assume that our lives are on hold until we do. Or if we don't have significant alignment between what we're good at and what we do for paid work every day, we may feel like we've missed it, that God's not speaking or that he calls other people but not us. But this is simply untrue. This thinking is not only problematic, it's also unbiblical.

So how should we understand calling? Author Quentin Schultze helps by suggesting two levels of calling. One is the calling or vocation shared by all followers of Jesus: to care for God's world and to be a blessing to others—to love God and neighbor. Borrowing from John Calvin, Schultze describes the other level as "each person's many *stations*—the particular places, relationships, and work in and through which a person cares." These stations are dynamic while our overall calling to Christ remains the same. Schultze says, "our calling is a lifelong process of connecting our shared vocation with our individual stations."[4]

When we think we have to find one "right" calling nugget in a deep river of choices, we may fail to steward our *here and now* lives for God. If we think instead in terms of faithfulness in each of our many stations, we can look and listen daily for ways to steward every area of our lives. We can listen for, discover and act on the good works God has uniquely prepared in advance for us (Ephesians 2:10) in our jobs, neighborhoods, relationships, leisure and everyday comings and goings.

WHAT AM I SUPPOSED TO BE WHEN I GROW UP?

We may feel pressure to know exactly what we want to do for our occupation when we graduate, but the reality is it can take *years* to discover. We may have no idea what we want to do, and we won't know until we try things. Once we start exploring we may find that we still have no clue. In college we receive a steady stream of performance feedback: our grades. They tell us what we're good at (or not). In our jobs it's unlikely that we'll have such constant feedback; therefore it can take a long time to learn what we're good at. It's normal to still feel directionless even after a few jobs. The twenties are for training, previewing and prototyping.[5] Take a deep breath and say, "It's okay if I don't know right away." And it's normal for things to change along the way. As Schultze says, "There is no single calling, one-track plan, or changeless career for our lives."[6]

In Courage and Calling, *Gordon Smith says not to fret if we're in our late twenties and still don't know what we want to do; most of us don't really know ourselves until we are in our midthirties.*[7]

It's also okay if we think we may know what we want to do but have yet to find a job that matches our education or interests. In a fluid economic time there's a good chance the job market may not offer a fit with our professional goals, or maybe not right away.[8] We may work that less-than-best job, take a gap year, volunteer, do an internship or pursue overseas missions for a stint. In fact, if we are able, one of the most shaping things we can do for our career path is to consider giving a year or two to service either locally or globally. Countless alumni share how their years of volunteerism or midterm missions service have influenced their current calling.

It's also normal to contemplate quitting a job. If you've graduated and you love your job, give thanks. But if you're just starting out in the job world and you think you need to quit, welcome to the club. As one alum puts it, the twenties are the "decade of angst." For many of us it's a time when we're constantly questioning, doubting and deliberating.

Today's recent graduates go through an average of seven job changes in their twenties, and "six in 10 have already changed careers at least once."[9]

Faye, a recent alum who landed her "dream job" right out of college, emailed recently with doubts. When she was hired as an electrical engineer for a building service, Faye was thrilled. They offered good compensation, she would get to use her gifts as an engineer and she loved the company's mission statement about continuing to learn and improve the world within the industry and beyond it. Faye anticipated ways she and her colleagues might leverage their talent to make a difference.

But even if we find a great fit, it's not a guarantee that our work will feel easy and meaningful every day. Eighteen months in, Faye shared that on many days her work feels like "paddling in place." She said, "There are quite too many times I wonder, is this job what I'm really meant to do? The difficulties and the mistakes I make seem to be a pointer for leaving them for someone else, because, if this job is really for me then how does it get so boring, uninspiring and hard? Am I missing out on something?" Faye admitted that her doubts doubled when another twenty-something coworker quit. He left to go skiing in the mountains. Faye wanted to know, "Am I missing out if I stay in cubical land instead of seeking the adventure life?"

These questions are normal! Especially right after college. In her classic novel *Their Eyes Were Watching God*, Zora Neale Hurston writes, "There are years that ask questions and years that answer."[10] We may feel like we have more questions than answers, and we may be unsure where to turn. Our days may start to feel meaningless, especially if we can't find answers right away or if it seems our "calling" eludes us. As we question *What should I be doing?* here are some realistic expectations:

- It's normal if we have no clue "what we want to be when we grow up."

- Even if we think we know, we may not be able to do that thing—yet.

- Even if we think we know now, that may change multiple times over our lives.

- If we don't feel a "sense of calling," it's okay. Our lives are not on hold until we do.

- Even if we find work in our field or an occupational fit, it's still normal to doubt.

- If we don't like our jobs (or can't find one), it's okay. We have multiple callings besides our paid worker role.

- We are *all* called in ways that are deep, wide, many and wonderful.

LIVING ON PURPOSE: WE'RE ALL CALLED

Discerning our calling implies a Caller. If we want to know our calling we need to know our Caller and what he's up to in the world. We need a story that accurately explains our world, God's role and our place. We find that story in the Bible, a plot that unfolds in four parts.

Creation: God created the world and *everything* in it, including us, his image-bearers. Life was sweet, and all things were in right relationship to each other—perfect order (Genesis 1:1, 31).

Fall: Sin entered in, bringing a curse to all of creation. The pain, suffering and mess we see around us—and in us—are the result of a perfect world distorted and broken by sin (Genesis 3:16-19).

Redemption: God sent Jesus to die and rise again to save us and the whole world from sin and death, to reverse the curse. God, through Jesus, is fixing our mess, and he invites us to join him in his work of making all things new! (Genesis 3:15; Isaiah 11; 53:2-6; Matthew 27).

Restoration: God is bringing his kingdom (perfect order) to every inch of this world, and we get to be a part of it! One day Christ will fully reign as rightful King over all; there will be no more tears, suffering, pain or death (Revelation 21:1-8; 22:1-3).

When we let this story permeate every area of our lives, we can view the world the way God sees it. This understanding should give us a reason to get up in the morning—even if we're confused about our career. Living into this story means we get to join Christ *daily*, wherever we are, in his ongoing work of caring for the whole creation: people, institutions, communities and the earth itself. Our purpose begins the moment we wake up and interact with the world. Whether the first person we see is our housemate, spouse or next-door neighbor, we start by serving people and looking for ways to bless them.

Our central call—the calling for all Christ-followers—is to hear and believe the gospel of Jesus Christ. Lee Hardy writes,

> In the New Testament the primary, if not exclusive, meaning of the term "vocation"—or calling (*klēsis*)—pertains to the call of the gospel, pure and simple. . . . Here we are not being asked to choose from a variety of callings, to decide which one is "right" for us. Rather, one call goes out to all—the call of discipleship. For it is incumbent upon all Christians to follow Christ, and, in so doing, to become the kind of people God wants us to be.[11]

We're called to respond to the gospel and to invite others to do likewise. As we respond by joining God in his work of restoring creation, we fulfill the Great Commission: to make disciples of all nations, baptize them and teach them to obey everything Christ has commanded (Matthew 28:18-20). We are *all called* to these things:

- To hear and believe the gospel (Romans 10:9)
- To love God and love others (Mark 12:28-34)
- To join God in making culture, cultivating the good creation (Genesis 1:26)
- To make disciples (Matthew 28:18-20)

- To obey everything God has commanded us (Exodus 20:1-20; Matthew 28:18-20)
- To be holy in all we do (1 Peter 1:15)
- To rest (Genesis 2:2; Exodus 20:8-11; Hebrews 4)
- To act justly, love mercy and walk humbly with our God (Micah 6:8)

Remember the promise given to the patriarch Abraham for him and all generations to follow? We are blessed by God to be a blessing to others. We live each day paying attention, serving and seeking the welfare of those around us (believers and unbelievers alike). Also, we approach life with a perspective that every station, every area of our lives matters—even the mundane parts like data entry, laundry and dishes. No matter what we're doing, we do it for the glory of God (1 Corinthians 10:31). This is missional, kingdom living. And this is a calling worth living for.

BLOOM AND PLANT WHERE PLANTED

We can live out our central, general calling no matter where we are or what we're doing for paid work. This is good news because only a small percentage of people do exactly what they're built for every day. Often we imagine a perfect match between passions and job as common. Or we assume that for those who have such overlap, life is easy all of the time.

There's that rare individual who from the time he was five has known he wanted to be a veterinarian when he grew up and then goes on to become just that! Then there's the rest of us. We have no clue what we want to be when we grow up, not to mention what to do for paid work now. As mentioned in chapter four, often when we ask *What's God's will for my life?* we expect God to drop out of the sky and tell us to do something grand: move to Calcutta, start a nonprofit or marry the person we like. Sometimes he does just that—he reveals himself so specifically that it can be nothing less than a clarion call from Christ himself. But from talking with many faithful Christians I've learned that such revelation moments are few and far between.

As Lee Hardy writes, "Discovering God's will for one's life is not so much a matter of seeking out miraculous signs and wonders as it is being attentive to who and where we are."[12] Rather than waiting for the extraordinary thing to be revealed, we can choose to live for Christ here and now. Faithfulness is less about hearing a call to become an overseas missionary and more about how we live each day for God's glory. Don't get me wrong, we need people who are courageous enough to follow a call to foreign missions. I in no way want to diminish those deep and true calls from God. In fact, some of us may need to be challenged to be more open to "going"—wherever that may be. However, for those who may be inclined to feel insignificant or stalled until we hear a call, we need to know that unless we're disobeying a word from God to go elsewhere, where we live *right now* is where we are *called*.

We can choose to bloom wherever we are planted and for whatever amount of time we are there. And if we're feeling more like Faith (directionless) or Faye (full of doubt), we can still "plant" when we're not feeling very bloomy. We can focus on what God may be doing in, around and through us, despite dissatisfaction. We can put down roots in our community, till the hard soil (sometimes in our own souls) and scatter seed. We can plant even when things look more gloomy than bloomy.[13]

MANY ROLES, MULTIPLE CALLINGS

If we let go of the idea of having one occupational calling in this life, we can focus on faithfulness in other roles. Work is good—but paid worker is not the only role we play. We have multiple callings within varied stations that change throughout life. For example, right now I am called to be a faithful employee, wife, mom, daughter, sister, friend and citizen. We should not be preparing just for a career, but rather for a lifetime of faithfulness in many different facets of life.

With a multifaceted approach we understand that it's not just about the job, but *who* we are and *how* we live while we're at work. If you asked my husband whether he feels called to be a graphic designer for a chromatography company, there's a good chance he'd say no. But if you asked him whether he gets to use his God-given gifts (art making, drawing, designing) each day to serve others, he'd say yes. He seeks to be faithful in his job—to show up on time and treat his colleagues with kindness and respect. He desires to do excellent design work and to build authentic relationships. He may not say he's "called" to his company, but he is called to be a faithful employee and coworker. This perspective allows him to bloom where planted in his workplace, neighborhood and home, living faithfully in many areas of life.

Even if we are able to say that we feel called to a certain type of work, there may be times when we need to put that work on hold because other callings take precedence. We may find ourselves newly married, putting our spouses' dreams and career aspirations above our own for a stretch. Or perhaps we decline a dream job so we can care for a sick family member or rear children.

Shortly after graduation, Terri found herself with one of the biggest calling questions of her life when her older sister suffered a life-changing brain injury.[14] Her sister was divorced, had a son and was "living a godless life with a 20-year history of drug and alcohol abuse." With both parents unfit to care for their daughter, Terri wrestled with her responsibility: "What [does] it mean to deny myself, pick up my cross and follow Christ? Move out of the state and take care of her? Or [is] that my selfish way to feel needed? . . . I [am] willing. But [is] that my calling?" After much prayer and counsel from a trusted mentor, Terri decided to move to care for her sister. When she looks back she sees "God's perfect timing" in the situation, but at the time her choice brought deep struggle, loneliness and pain. It cost her. While the world told her, "take care of yourself" and "pursue your dreams," Terri sacrificed to pursue the calling of caregiver to someone else. Sometimes we choose things that are not best for us personally but are best for a family member, spouse or child. There are many important roles to play, including sibling, spouse and parent.

In a TED talk Emilie Wapnick critiques the concept of "one true calling," arguing that there are individuals who will never be able to pick just one thing—not because they are indecisive, but because they have multiple talents and passions. They are "multipotentialites" or "multipods." In this economic time, multipods may find themselves better equipped to adjust to an ever-changing job market because of their nimbleness.[15]

DISCERNING OUR PERSONAL GIFTS, PASSIONS AND POTENTIAL JOB FIT

My friend Beth is a chemistry professor, and despite hard days she enjoys great overlap between her occupation and vocation. She traces the stirrings of her professional calling back to age ten. She was watching a news feature that displayed an image of the IBM logo in blue dots on a gray background, while a scientist talked about how each dot was an individual atom. Fascinated, Beth exclaimed, "Mom, Mom! Did you know we can see atoms?" She has maintained this childlike wonder, and she finds that in the field of nanoscience she can explore the beauty of God's creation—perhaps even seeing something never observed before.

Beth also points to a pivotal conversation with one of her professors when she was a student. At the time she was taking her most difficult course yet, physical chemistry, and it caused her to question her career path and calling:

The class had rattled my world to the degree that I was dreaming of quitting college. I was torn between an others-centered desire to move to Africa to work with orphans and a self-centered desire to move to the beach and work as a waitress. It was within this angst that I had to schedule a meeting with my physical chemistry lab professor to have a lab report editing session.

Beth arrived for chemistry help, but when her inner turmoil came spilling out, her professor offered much more. As she discussed the two career options she was considering (orphan care versus waitressing), he respectfully asked whether she could identify specific ways that God was calling her to move to Africa or the beach. When she told him these ideas mainly came from her internal angst, he started talking about Moses.

The professor explained that Moses was likely going about his ordinary day when he noticed the burning bush. He wasn't actively seeking direction, but God chose to appear to him in an unexpected way. It was when Moses stepped aside that God spoke to him. The professor encouraged Beth to stay open as she went about her day, looking for "burning bushes" and responding to those moments by asking God what he wanted to show her. Because, as poet Elizabeth Barrett Browning put it, if we're paying attention, "every common bush [is] afire."[16] The ordinary is the extraordinary.

As Beth looks back, she sees that discerning calling has been about "stepping aside" to the countless little moments that affirmed next steps for her: finishing her degree, heading to graduate school and eventually accepting a college-level teaching position. Throughout her twenties Beth received affirmation of her giftedness as a chemist and teacher, but there were still days when she contemplated a completely different career (such as children's ministry director). In the end it came down to stewarding the gifts that God opened up for her as she journeyed with him. While she pursued her doctoral degree in chemistry God blessed her with opportunities that she could have never imagined, and she desired to steward her education and experience for him. Her daily work is not easy, but she believes God has called her to her particular work at this particular time. She has found (one of) her calling(s)—for now.

As we discern what we should do with our lives and how and where to serve God with our gifts, here are some practices from Beth's story and others' that we can apply to our own process.

Listen. In a world that silences God's call, we need to learn how to listen for the ways he speaks. How is God speaking to his creation, and how has he spoken over time? As we reflect on some of the most compelling stories of hearing (Abraham, Moses, Samuel, Elijah, Isaiah, the prophets speaking to Israel, the call of the disciples and so on), what can we observe? How will we step aside in our everyday lives to hear God?

Look back. We may go as far back as our childhood and remember days when we lined up our stuffed animals to "teach" them, started a small business in our neighborhood, stayed up all night reading or writing a story, or had an "Aha!" discovery moment. What do our past experiences tell us about our current interests, gifts and passions? We can also look back on places of suffering or pain as well as places of God's faithfulness to us. How might a past experience reveal a future step?

Pay attention. In *Visions of Vocation*, Steven Garber urges us to pay attention—to have eyes to see and ears to hear. What do we notice about ourselves and our world? What captures our imagination? Keeps us up at night? Makes us cry? What injustice do we want to see made right? When we pay attention, we more fully understand our world, our place in it and our responsibility to make it better. Garber asks, "Knowing what you know about yourself and the world, what are you going to do?"[17] We find our calling when we "see [our]selves as implicated in the way the world is and ought to be."[18]

Let others speak. Others may know us better than we know ourselves. We discover our calling in community, and our output to the world is never about just us. We may ask our friends and family: What am I good at? What do you think I should try? We should allow others to call out our gifts and develop our potential. When I was a college senior a close friend said, "You love Jesus and you love college. You should consider campus ministry." I dismissed it at the time (mostly because I thought it would require raising personal support), but that comment came back to me years later when I was discerning whether or not to apply to the organization I now work for. God spoke through others who knew me best to land me where I am today.

Try stuff! It would be nice if we could take an online test or drop by the career center and find our perfect fit. But any career counselor worth her salt would say that one of the best avenues to discovery is exploration—we need to try stuff! We need to preview and prototype. When we can try something at a low risk, we begin to discover our interests and gifts. So take that unpaid internship, volunteer, job shadow or do an informational interview. If you think you might want to become a pediatric speech pathologist, find out what a day in the life of one is like.

Assessments can be a good starting place, but they are often most helpful when our results are applied to contexts where we are doing things.

As we try things, we need to tell ourselves, *It's okay to fail.* It's fine to figure out that we're not good at something or that we don't enjoy something—even if we just spent four years studying it. God is not going to waste any experience. Over my years in college ministry, we have had numerous interns who join our staff in order to discern whether they want to go into full-time ministry. Some quickly discover that college ministry is not a fit, others figure out that they miss aspects of their former job or field (like Andrea, who returned to special education after a year), while others feel "This is what I've been made to do!" (like Mike, who now gives leadership to much of the operations of our ministry). We don't know until we try, and the twenties are the years to explore!

CONCLUSION

If we're wondering what we should be doing, whether we should quit our job or how we can steward our God-given gifts, we can take comfort in the fact that we are part of a much bigger story than our own little, messy and confusing lives. There may be days of boredom, months of doubt, years of lacking direction and even decades of angst. But our small lives are not too insignificant for God and his world. It all matters.

It was that reminder that kept Faye from quitting, grabbing some skis and heading for the mountains. At the time she needed perspective most, she found it among fellow Christian engineers—who normalized her specific struggles—and within her faith community. Faye recently emailed,

> I know every day matters to God and that my job is exactly where I need to focus and dedicate myself in service. My job can suck, but this job is teaching me many things to prepare me for the next part of the story God is telling with my life—a story that will take my lifetime to tell. And suddenly, administrative work seems less like getting stuck in the middle of nowhere.

Faye no longer paddles in place but sees her everyday faithfulness as part of her role in a much bigger story—the story of her own life and the grand story of the Caller's work in the world.

GOING DEEPER

1. What comes to mind when you hear the word *calling*? How have you defined it, and would you change anything about your current definition?

2. What are some of the roles you play or stations you steward right now? How can you pursue faithfulness in each?

3. How do you hear God's voice? What makes it hard to hear? Is there anything you hear him saying right now?

4. As you pay attention to the world, what do you notice? Knowing what you know about yourself and the world, what are you going to do?

5. Imagine for a bit: If money were no object, what's your dream job? If it's not your current reality, are there career steps that may get you closer? Or are there ways you can explore your dream through other life stations?

6. What is something you want to try that might help you discern your gifts, passions or job fit?

Scripture study: Genesis 1:26; Micah 6:8; Matthew 28:18-20; 1 Corinthians 1:9; 10:31; Ephesians 2:10; Hebrews 4; 1 Peter 1:15

Recommended reading:

Steven Garber, *Visions of Vocation: Common Grace for the Common Good.* Downers Grove, IL: InterVarsity Press, 2014.

Quentin Schultze, *Here I Am: Now What on Earth Should I Be Doing?* Grand Rapids: Baker Books, 2005.

Gordon Smith, *Courage and Calling: Embracing Your God-Given Potential.* Rev. ed. Downers Grove, IL: InterVarsity Press, 2011.

ELEVEN

A FAITH THAT WORKS

ADJUSTING TO OUR JOBS,
CONNECTING THEM TO CHRIST

*The significance—and ultimately the quality—of the work
we do is determined by our understanding of the
story in which we are taking part.*

WENDELL BERRY, *CHRISTIANITY AND
THE SURVIVAL OF CREATION*

DURING HER COLLEGE YEARS AMELIA worked harder than most of her costume design major peers. She skipped football games, stitched over Christmas breaks and prayed for a job in which she could be a blessing to others. When she pictured herself in that first job, she envisioned making great costumes and having many gospel conversations. She desperately wanted to serve God, and she believed her hard work and steadfast prayer would pay off. Eager to launch into her career, Amelia accepted her first offer: an entry-level position as a stitcher for a theater company in New York City.

Then reality hit. Her first day was awful, and it only declined from there. She quickly noticed a disparity between generations of employees. Some of her older coworkers, including her boss, demeaned younger workers. They reminded Amelia of her place with comments like "Don't touch the photocopier" or by bringing an egg timer to clock her ten-minute break. Amelia, who had no intention of making copies or stealing company time, felt patronized. It seemed each day brought another incident of employee mistreatment, such as the time her boss called a number of workers into her office and fired one of them in front of everyone present. Amelia, who entered her job dreaming of making a difference, instead found herself crying in the stairwell every day. Is this what work is meant to be? As she bumped up against the realities of her workplace, Amelia began to question the meaning of work, her faith and her calling.

Though our workplace may not present the same struggles, there's a good chance there will be something about our work that causes us to doubt or question. We may ask:

- What's the point if we don't like our job?
- What does it mean to live faithfully at work?
- How do we share verbally about our faith at work (or, should we)?
- Does the workweek have the same value as the weekend?

Our understanding of why we work and our job expectations will significantly shape our transition into the world of work.

OUR PERCEPTIONS AND CULTURE'S PERSPECTIVE ON WORK

I have a friend who shares the same Facebook post every Friday: "TGIF!" In many ways we live in a Thank-God-It's-Friday world where work is something we get through in order to enjoy the weekend. Though there's nothing wrong with relishing the changed pace of a lazy Saturday, we need to ask ourselves what we believe about the rest of the week—the forty plus hours we spend at our job. Is work just a means to the weekend?

Our culture tells us that *work is a necessary evil*. Though we, like Amelia, may set out with hopes of finding meaningful work and making a contribution to the world, when we don't love our first job or we're still waiting for a better offer (or any offer!), we can start to question the point of work. We can easily adopt the culture's attitude: work is something to slog through so we can do what we really want to do—relax, binge on Netflix or vacation.

If we view work as drudgery, it shapes *how* we work. One of the greatest challenges we may encounter is the temptation to coast. Many recent alumni struggle to see the value in their work, so they get by in their job; the workweek is simply a means to the weekend. When one alum, Sam, was asked about his faith challenges in entering the marketplace, he talked about coasting: "We look forward to vacation or retirement instead of glory. . . . When we forget our purpose, our goal pretty quickly becomes comfort."[1]

On the one hand our culture tells us work is simply a means to an end, while on the other hand it tempts us to view our paid work as the ultimate measure of self. Our position and earning potential become a mark by which to measure our worth. If you haven't already gone, you'll likely be invited soon to your five-year high school reunion. If you opt to attend, the first question people will likely ask is, "What do you do?" Certainly we're curious about what fills someone's day, but we also size each other up, and sadly we make judgments about each other based on how much money we make.

When we draw our strength and worth from work rather than God, we turn work into an idol. We feel tempted to overwork and prove ourselves. Though a strong work ethic is crucial, an ideology that has us working eighty hours a week with unhealthy motivations is not what God intends. One alum wants to know, "Where does work end and life begin?" Another says, "I don't want my career to consume me. I want to succeed, but I don't want it to be for selfish reasons."

Lexi shares her life-work challenges as a first-time teacher in an ethnically diverse school district. Beyond the steep learning curve, lack of performance feedback, language barrier and failing students, she struggled to know when to stop working each day:

> I spent really long hours. I would stay up until like 11 pm, and then I would get up really early the next day, come in and then do the same thing the next night. Learning boundaries was the trickiest part for me. You can't do everything 100%. I thought, "if I just work harder, I can get it done," but I realized I could never work hard enough. That was really hard to adjust to—to not knowing when to be done.

We can't do it all. Joyce Jarek, author of *First Job*, hopes that every recent graduate can understand that "you don't have to be perfect every day at everything."[2] Watching many first-time employees become anxious, unsettled and worn down by trying to do it all, she encourages new hires to not be too hard on themselves and to restore balance in time instead of trying to find perfect balance in each day. For example, we may work extra hours in one week, but we follow that stretch by a changed rhythm in the next. We cannot sustain long periods of over-working (or time off, for that matter) without restoring balance.

The temptation to overwork is real, and so is the temptation to coast. So how do we view work with right perspective? Is work a blessing or curse? Is it just something that pays the bills so we can do what we really want? Or is there something more?

DEVELOPING A BIBLICAL PERSPECTIVE OF WORK

We desperately need God's view on work—especially as we make the huge transition from the role of student to worker. "The significance—and ultimately the quality—of the work we do is determined by our understanding of the story in which we are taking part."[3] A weather reporter memorizes the map before she stands in front of the green screen; her knowledge of the backdrop informs the movements she makes. If she doesn't know the backdrop, her gestures become senseless. The same is true for us and our work. When we know the grand back-story—the context for our work—we know *how* to approach our work.[4]

The Bible opens with the book of Genesis, whose name means "book of beginnings." From the start of our story we learn that *God commands work* (Genesis 1:28; 2:15) and that *we are made in God's image, the image of a worker* (Genesis 1:26-27). God's immediate in-structions to Adam and Eve are to cultivate the earth and take care of it—go work. God charges us to be workers, inviting us to join him as cocreators. When we design, build, engineer, help, create, heal, serve, protect and improve our world in ways that honor God, we continue the good work he began at the start of creation.

As the biblical story unfolds, in those first few chapters of Genesis and through to Revelation, we glean three principles that shape our understanding of work:

1. Work has been created good.

2. Work is fallen.

3. Work is being redeemed.

Work is good. *Work—in and of itself—is inherently good and spiritual.* Though our culture tries to convince us that work is a necessary evil, what we learn from Genesis 1 is that work exists pre-fall. Before sin appears, God declares work a good thing. We tend to place value on work only if we have something significant to say about it (such as, I got to share the gospel with my coworker) or if there's some "spiritual" component of the day, but work itself is inherently good and spiritual. Simply keeping the biblical command to go work glorifies God. We delight in opportunities to verbally share our faith, but that is not the measure of the worth of our work.

Nor is one type of job more valuable than another. With the exception of certain profane or immoral lines of work (dealing drugs, prostitution, sex trade and so on), we need faithful Christians in all sectors of society. Though we may have been taught to think God has a hierarchy of careers (with missionaries, pastors or "full-time ministers" at the top), this could not be further from the truth![5] We are losing our Christian influence in many streams of culture because we're opting out of places including Hollywood, politics and sciences.[6]

On the flipside, we also see recent alumni who do not view full-time vocational missions as a valuable and viable work option, especially if it requires raising personal funds. Recent graduates are declining opportunities in crucial lines of work. Whatever our hang-ups, let's not automatically say no for any career option. All jobs are high callings.

As we prepared for a day of discussing faith and the workplace, Lin commented, "It seems to me that what I am about to do has nothing to do with God's kingdom, which makes me sad." After our time together, though, her view began to shift. As an international relations major, Lin started to see the ways her field relates to God's kingdom as she builds bridges between cultures, fosters communication and works toward making peace—all priorities of Jesus. When we think that a kingdom perspective means reducing work to just a few jobs we deem worthy, then we've missed the kind of kingdom Christ is bringing and the king himself.

Work is fallen. In Genesis 3, we learn that work becomes toil (vv. 17-19). Like everything else in creation, work is subjected to the curse. Work—this side of heaven—will not fully satisfy us. Our companies are broken, our nonprofits are broken and our Christian organizations are broken. We are broken. We will feel the brokenness and toil in our work when our employer treats us poorly, when we strive for approval, when we experience frustration with a coworker or a project deadline. Our jobs will be toil, sweat and pain at times. But our toil is *not* in vain (1 Corinthians 15:58).

The toil Amelia experienced in her first job ultimately led her to quit. Though I caution recent graduates against walking away too quickly, it is possible that leaving a job may be the most faithful move we can make. Author Al Hsu writes,

> While it is true that all work is potentially meaningful and significant, it is not true that all work is equally strategic. Some work may in fact be immoral or irrelevant. If a job seems meaningless and we don't discern that our presence there is of any long-term benefit to either the company and other people or our own well-being . . . these may well be indications that we should pursue other opportunities.[7]

For Amelia, quitting was a necessary step. She regrets that she stayed for a year before finding the strength and freedom to leave.

We will need to determine if we should leave or persevere. Sometimes, much of the "toil" in our first jobs comes from adjusting to a new position. One alum, Jasmine, shares her insecurities when her company hired her for a full-time role after her internship. She felt unprepared and inadequate to perform the responsibilities of the new role. She constantly compared herself to others, especially when supervising people only a few months younger or much older. Her projects and tasks differed from her education and training, which only brought more anxiety. Within time, though, Jasmine began to realize that God wanted to meet her in these challenges—to offer her grace and strength in her weakness. As she placed her fear and incompetency before him, God gave her "freedom from anxiety" and an ability to "leave [her] work at work" as she trusted him to take care of it.

Work is being redeemed! Christ is making *all* things right, including our work (Colossians 1:20). He is returning work to the joy it was intended to be in Eden and will be in the new heavens and new earth (Isaiah 65:22-23; Revelation 21). Yes, we will work in heaven! But it will be perfect—without toil, temptation, helplessness or disappointment.

As we anticipate what work will be like when the kingdom fully comes, we must ask ourselves here and now: How will we live in our professions? How will we reflect what we believe about the way work ought to be?

I love to hear stories of how our alumni dedicate themselves to living out this redemption in their jobs. Curt believes every child deserves access to quality education. He currently teaches fourth grade, serving students in an under-resourced district. Brock, an investigative journalist for a city newspaper, commits to telling honest, fair stories despite the pressure to slant and slander. Asia, a personal trainer, imagines a world without an obesity epidemic and expensive interventions that rob quality of life; she wants to be part of promoting health and fitness practices that allow us to honor our bodies and enjoy life. Faye and Robert, both engineers, desire to see their communities flourish because of the good design work of their companies. Though they have small parts in a bigger whole, they both seek to engineer with integrity, even in the smallest tasks. When we commit ourselves to the values of peace, beauty, safety, justice, joy, wholeness, economic flourishing and care for the environment, our redemptive work becomes a part of the coming kingdom![8]

As we consider the basic biblical principles of work being good, fallen and redeemed, we should be mindful of the ways we see this pattern in our own line of work. *What about your field or area of study is good? What's fallen? Where do you see opportunity for redemption?*

We will discuss this further, but when it comes to living faithfully in the workplace, here are some rails to run on:

- We see our job as a sacred, good gift.
- We worship God simply by going to work.
- We seek to glorify God in every aspect—in *how* we work.
- We're aware of ways work is fallen, and we seek to be part of redeeming it.
- We seek first to bless the people around us (instead of trying to convert them).

FAITH CONVERSATIONS AT WORK

Some alumni think that "living out our faith at work" means we have to have a gospel conversation. If we see no inherent good in work itself, but place value on it *only* if we get to share our faith verbally with coworkers, then we've missed the deep and wide vision God has for our work. That said, we don't want to minimize the opportunity to be a witness through our words. If our faith affects every area of our lives, then we don't need to compartmentalize it when we're at work.

So how do we share our faith verbally at work? First, our strongest witness is our faithfulness to the work at hand. When we do our job, arrive on time and treat our colleagues with love and respect, we garner trust and influence in the workplace. Choosing to live differently and to operate with integrity on every level will set us apart. One alum challenges our seniors every year to make a commitment to avoid gossip. Knowing the incredible temptation to succumb to talking about others, he encourages recent graduates to decide from day one to resist the gossip culture.

Jeremiah 29:7 says, "Seek the peace and prosperity of the city . . . because if it prospers, you too will prosper." When we seek *first* to bless the people and place where God has us, God will open doors for us to share our faith. Pray for the success of your company, your leaders and your colleagues (especially the ones who annoy you the most). Bring your coworkers before Jesus in prayer before trying to take Jesus to your coworkers.

Author and entrepreneur Mark Russell shares a story of two call centers in Thailand. In one, the Christian workers focused on trying to *convert* their nonbelieving colleagues—making evangelistic conversations paramount. In the other, Christians sought to *bless* their coworkers—seeking the welfare of the employees and the flourishing of the center at large. The result: the "blessers" saw their coworkers come to saving faith in a ratio that far surpassed their "converter" counterparts—forty-eight to one! We are blessed to be a blessing. As we live that out, God moves![9]

When Amelia reflects on her desire to be a blessing, she admits that though she had a genuine desire to love her coworkers, she was hoping to get some personal satisfaction out of it too. She recognizes that her initial picture was naive and her motivation for blessing others was more about how it would make her feel than what would actually benefit her coworkers. In her current job with a different company she still wants to bless her coworkers, but she approaches it with a new perspective. She says, "I'm there, prepared to be a blessing, but not forcing it on others." She's more open minded, trusting God to move. "God is going to use me as needed in ways that are good for the people around me. I can let go." On a practical level, Amelia talks about the importance of getting a good night's sleep before work (versus the unhealthy habits she kept in her first job). Many of her coworkers have had negative experiences with Christians, so she wants to be on her toes, prepared in mind and body.

I wish I could offer a five-step formula for how to have gospel conversations in the workplace, but the move of God cannot be reduced to a cookie-cutter method, nor can one practice cover every work context. Inevitably there will be times when we say too little—when we have the opportunity to witness to what we have seen God do in our lives, but we keep our mouths shut. Other times we may say too much. Maybe we're spouting off some faith principle, but we're not even living it ourselves. Or perhaps we're not properly honoring our work time or place. We need to be mindful of our context and maintain integrity in how we use our company's hours.

If you feel the tension of trying to share your faith without forcing it on someone, that's probably a healthy sign. Life is full of tensions to be managed, and the moment we stop feeling the tension, there's a good chance we have fallen off to one side or the other. As we manage the tension we should surround ourselves with others who can help—older mentors, friends and especially one or two coworkers (if possible) who share our faith.

My prayer is that you don't reduce your work to an evangelism platform, but at the same time you live *on mission*, trusting God to provide open doors and the faith to step through them.

ADJUSTING TO THE WORLD OF WORK

As we anticipate those first days on our new job, there are some practical things we can do to prepare. Much of our adjustment will have to do with the attitudes and actions we adopt, and those practices we put in place early on can significantly shape our approach for years to come. Here are some principles to consider.

Manage expectations. Expectations for that first job are often either sky high or way too low. For those of us wanting to land our dream job, we may find our hopes deferred when a job is not all we imagined it would be. We may find we are not as competent as we hoped—that we lack the skills we need to actually do the job or we know less about the job market than we thought. Or perhaps we have ideas about how we want to see transformation in our workplace, but our low position doesn't allow us to make sweeping change (right now). Maybe we're unprepared for the office politics or gossip or upper-leadership decision making. We may be surprised by how little performance feedback we receive, or on the other hand maybe we're shocked by how closely we're watched—how little autonomy we seem to have. Perhaps we're simply unprepared to relate to coworkers who are much older or whose thoughts and perspectives differ from ours.

When high expectations go unmet or when we view our job as insignificant, a "whatever job," it can be easy to write off a certain stretch until we reach the next thing—the thing we're really hoping for. But let me encourage you to see the benefits of a job that isn't an ideal fit, or even of a season of unemployment. For example, one alum who works as a barista shared that though this is not what she pictured herself doing, she has more free time than most of her peers and is able to read books by authors she's always wanted to dive into, such as

Bonhoeffer and Nouwen. Another alum told how his time waiting tables not only turned him into a better tipper, but also gave him an unexpected leadership opportunity when he was quickly moved into a management role—an experience that shaped him for future leadership in a different organization.

Take the long view. It's important to keep in mind that the twenties are training ground. We need to take the long view. When we put in time at the entry level, God can shape us for an ideal fit. We can choose to practice patience and humility. Robert, reflecting on the things he learned in his first job, shared, "Even if the work you are handed as a beginner seems incredibly menial or trivial, give it your best shot, and do it from an attitude of humility and patience." When we demonstrate a positive spirit and effectiveness in our present jobs, we set ourselves up for a promising future.

Own your adjustment. As we transition into the workplace, it's important to take personal responsibility for our adjustment rather than expecting our employer or coworkers to acclimate us. Hopefully we will receive some basic orientation, but I'm talking about parts of the transition that supersede the location of the copy machine or even office policies. We need to acclimate to our new setting rather than expecting the workplace to adjust to us and our preferences. Our attitude, actions and even attire will make an impact on how we're perceived by others. From day one, let's make choices that allow others to see us as we hope to be viewed rather than reinforce a stereotype we want to avoid.

Operate with integrity. Our work ethic and the way in which we treat others (especially those who have been with the employer for years before we arrived) is crucial. And again, humility is key. You are the new person. Take time to truly learn the work culture before you try to change it. Our integrity, etiquette and the way we navigate interactions with upper leadership may make or break our experience. Our pursuit of faithfulness in the little things—such as not stealing office supplies or checking personal email or social media—prepares us to practice integrity in all areas—such as the way we talk about coworkers even in the midst of temptation or how we treat people in the face of a deadline.

Clarify values. Allow these years to acquaint you with the world of work so you can appropriately clarify your values. As we get out there, we may find that we fit better with a certain work culture. Perhaps you prefer a more fixed setting than a fluid one. Or we may learn that our values don't align with a certain company or institution. For example, your convictions about environmental stewardship will not allow you to work with X company because of their disregard for ecological issues. Though Christians are needed in every line of work, the day in and day out decisions of workplace fit are nuanced; discerning fit is more complex than saying any Christian should be able to work anywhere as long as the line of work is legal.

For example, I know an alum, Joel, who chose to step away from a well-paid comptroller position because he was asked to falsify numbers. When he confronted his boss, he dismissed Joel's concerns, saying, "No one asked you to be the inner conscience of this company." Joel wrestled with what to do, but ultimately decided he could not compromise his ethics and found the courage to quit. Another alum, Scott, faces challenges in his competitive marketing job when asked to work on ads that compromise his views on human worth and sexuality. Despite his best creative efforts to turn things in a different direction, he wonders: can I stay with this company? Understanding the marketplace and clarifying our values within it are key parts of our work development. Give yourself grace and patience as you discern and pray.

Resist temptation. Because the world of work is teeming with opportunities to love God and serve others, the enemy wants to tempt and derail us. We need to be ever mindful of the temptation to make work about what we can gain from it rather than about the goodness of work itself. We will be tempted by money, power, approval (needing to be liked or needed) and security.[10] We must keep these temptations in check and seek a higher view of work—where it's not about our benefit but God's glory.

As we manage expectations, take the long view, own our adjustment, operate with integrity, clarify values and resist temptation, we begin to connect our work to the greater story—the good work that God is doing in us, through us and in the world. Hopefully this leads us to finding meaning and purpose in our labor.

Despite a bumpy start into the work world, Amelia loves her current job as an assistant costume designer for a smaller, competitive production company. When asked why, she talks about having the autonomy to make decisions, being competent at what she's doing, feeling a sense of purpose when making good art and receiving fair compensation. She lacked all of these in her first job. But now, on good days, bad days, slow or no-progress days, even on days her designer decides not to use her finely stitched dress (that took weeks to make), Amelia finds joy and meaning. God has given her good work, and she desires to be faithful in every part of it.

In his book Drive, *Daniel Pink identifies three essential work motivators: autonomy, mastery and purpose.*[11]

If we want to honor God in every aspect of our work, we must know that our fulfillment comes from him alone. He is the one who gives us a right view of work, who provides work itself and who gives us opportunities to love and serve others through our work. May our entire work lives be an act of worship unto him, and may this prayer of Moses become our prayer:

> Satisfy us in the morning with your unfailing love,
>   that we may sing for joy and be glad all our days. . . .
> May the favor of the Lord our God rest on us;
>   establish the work of our hands for us—
>   yes, establish the work of our hands. (Psalm 90:14, 17)

GOING DEEPER

1. What are your perceptions of work? Do they differ from the dominant cultural messages (work is a necessary evil or work is the ultimate measure of a person)?

2. What does the biblical story say about work? How can you apply one key scriptural insight to your current job or work search?

3. What is your perspective when it comes to sharing your faith verbally at work? What do you need to pray about most right now?

4. How can you bless your coworkers or work environment? What is one thing you can do this week to prepare yourself to be used by God?

5. What have been, or what do you anticipate will be, the most challenging adjustments to the world of work? How can you prepare to navigate them?

6. What tempts you the most: money, power, approval or security? Why? How will you resist these temptations?

Scripture study: Genesis 1–3; Luke 4:8; 1 Corinthians 15:58; Colossians 3:23; 2 Thessalonians 3:10; 1 Peter 3:15

Recommended reading:

Joyce Jarek, *First Job: A Personal Career Guide for Graduates* (Victoria, BC: Friesen, 2014).

Timothy Keller with Katherine Leary Alsdorf, *Every Good Endeavor: Connecting Your Work to God's Work*, reprint ed. (New York: Penguin, 2014).

Tom Nelson, *Work Matters: Connecting Sunday Worship to Monday Work* (Wheaton, IL: Crossway, 2011).

TWELVE

FINANCIAL FAITHFULNESS

MANAGING MONEY

You may be rich or poor...

But you're gonna have to serve somebody.

BOB DYLAN, "GOTTA SERVE SOMEBODY"

HERE ARE SOME STATEMENTS ON FINANCES. Take a moment to decide whether the following are true or false.

- According to the Bible, money is the root of all evil.

- If you buy a $200,000 home (with a 20 percent down payment) at a 5 percent interest rate and pay it back over thirty years, you will actually pay over $300,000 to own that home.

- A car payment is unavoidable for recent graduates.

- The average consumer spends 12 to 18 percent more when paying with a credit card versus cash.

- Ann saves $200 per month, starting at age 18 and stopping at age 28

($24,000 saved). John saves $200 per month, starting at age 28 and stopping at age 65 ($88,000 saved). Both average 10 percent in annual interest until age 65. Because of *compound interest*, Ann has $1.4 million and John has $870,000.[1] (See note for the answers to these true/false statements.)

We rarely go through a day without spending, talking about or thinking about money. This is especially true after college. Whether we're adjusting to a new cost of living, trying to pay bills or tuition loans without a steady job, or managing more money than ever before, this next phase is full of financial challenges, changes and choices. The money decisions we make early on have the potential to significantly shape our trajectory for years to come. If we want to set our feet on a straight and steady course, we must know the obstacles we are up against and the opportunities that await us. We need perspective, tools and a game plan.

MONEY: ROOT OF ALL EVIL OR TICKET TO HAPPINESS?

When asked about the greatest challenges after college so far, Lynette shares, "Finances are always an issue." With the decisions she needs to make regarding loan payments, other debt and amounting bills, she concludes, "I hate money." Life would be easier if she didn't have to think about finances. Lynette, like many others who are overwhelmed with their current circumstance or the world's pressures, has adopted this perspective: money is the root of all evil. The issue with this attitude is that it is not only unbiblical, but it allows money to control us rather than the other way around. One of the most misquoted Bible verses is 1 Timothy 6:10: "For the *love* of money is a root of all kinds of evil" (emphasis mine). It's not the money but rather what we do with it—our relationship to it—that makes all the difference. Though managing money requires hard work, discipline and perseverance, money *itself* is not the root of evil.[2]

While some recent graduates hold money talk at arms' length, others run hard in a different direction—they chase the dollar, believing that

money will bring happiness. In obvious and subtle ways, they are consumed with the idea that life is about money. They fixate on increasing
their income and believe if they just had a little more, they would be
content. Like those who hate money, these individuals are also con-
trolled by riches (or the desire for them), just in a different way. Buying
the lie that personal affluence brings fulfillment, they have fallen into
a gaping pitfall: the love of money.

Neither loving money nor loathing it leads to a healthy perspective.
We need to look at money through the lens of Scripture, but first we
need to know what we're up against.

OUR CULTURE AND MONEY

We are messed up when it comes to money. We live in a culture where
money is an idol and debt is a way of life. As I write this, the US
government has exceeded eighteen trillion dollars in national debt and
Greece has received its third bailout in five years.[3] In the United
States, the average household consumer debt for those who carry a
balance on their credit cards is over $15,779.[4] Globally, nationally and
in our own homes we struggle to manage finances.

Our culture offers poor models when it comes to money management, and it also tells us to chase affluence. The advertising industry
lures us with its formula: you're not satisfied because you lack something, we have the thing you lack, spend your money on it and you will
be fulfilled. Even the most discerning of us are not entirely immune
to the effects of advertising or the claws of consumerism. The message
that money will buy contentment is everywhere, tantalizing us daily
with its lie.

The pressure for college students and recent graduates may be even
more intense. Think about it. Why did you come to college? Nearly
seventy-five percent of students agree that "the chief benefit of college
is that it increases one's earning power." Making more money has
become the number one reason for attending college, a vast change

from decades ago when students went to college to develop a "philosophy of life."[5] For many, the justification for higher education is exactly what the image on the best-selling college poster promotes: a mansion on a hill with a five-car garage filled with expensive sports cars.

Earning money is not wrong or bad, and I'd be the first to argue that a college education should have an end game connected to a viable career; but if earning money is the chief end of education, then what does that mean for leadership, citizenship and service? Does college have no bearing on the making of character? Sadly, many of us value our earning potential more than the shape of our souls.

GOTTA SERVE SOMEBODY: OUR MONEY MANAGEMENT REVEALS OUR VALUES

If you want to know what someone cares about, just take a look at their bank statement or credit card bill. What does our spending, giving or savings tell us about ourselves? Does our money management (or lack thereof) show that we are blessed to be a blessing? How?

We all need to decide whom we will serve: God or money? Jesus says, "No one can serve two masters. Either you will hate the one and love the other, or you will be devoted to the one and despise the other. You cannot serve both God and money" (Matthew 6:24). Bob Dylan had it right when he sang, "You're gonna have to serve somebody." We all worship something. The enemy will do all he can to corrupt our hearts when it comes to money. If money has a grip on us, we release that grip by loving God more than money. How? We become sacrificial. If we love money more than God, we let go by giving generously.

We also need to assess our heart attitudes. Do we hold our finances with open hands, knowing that it's all God's, or do we try to hold money closely, like a security blanket? Are we cheerful givers? As we are blessed with resources, do we simply raise our standard of living or do we raise our standard of giving? Jesus says, "Do not store up for yourselves treasures on earth . . . but store up for yourselves treasures in heaven. . . . For where your treasure is, there your heart will be also" (Matthew 6:19-21). What do you treasure? What's important to you? Our money choices reveal our deepest values.

Being faithful with our finances means that we not only get our hearts and minds in the right place, but we also dedicate ourselves to the discipline of stewardship. In the same way that a trustee takes responsibility for a property, business or organization for an authority figure's benefit, we are God's caretakers when it comes to money. Money is a provision, a gift from God; we get to honor, glorify and worship him by how we use it. Failing to manage our money shows that we don't take God's Word and our responsibility seriously.

Some people argue that if we really trust God, we shouldn't make a plan with our money. This attitude is irresponsible and not biblical. Though God delights when we trust him in sacrificial giving, he also instructs that we should "know the condition of [our] flocks" (Proverbs 27:23). In an agrarian society, shepherds diligently kept track of their animals because their livelihood depended on it. They looked for disease, managed threats and took tender care of livestock. Attentiveness to their herds had present and future implications. The same is true for us and our finances. When we pay attention, plan, save, give and live on a budget, we honor God.

BUDGET BASICS AND BREAKDOWN

We should pray for God to show us how he wants us to direct the money that comes through our hands or what we have in the bank. If we do not tell our money where to go, it will likely slip through our fingers without us realizing where it went! The best way to direct our dollars is to make a budget plan. This section will explain a typical budget breakdown as well as approximate percentages to plan on for each line item (see table 1).[6]

Keep in mind that at the end of the month our outgoing funds (expenses) should not exceed our incoming funds (salary/income).

These percentages are just guidelines, but if we spend on the high end of each percentage, we'll come in over budget, and that number doesn't even include the most important first step: tithe and offerings.

Table 1. Sample budget form

Budget Item	Percentage	Amount Budgeted	Amount Spent
Tithe and offerings			
Savings and debt	5-10%		
Housing and utilities	25-38%		
Auto/transportation	12-15%		
Household	15-25%		
Entertainment	5-10%		
Insurance	5%		
Miscellaneous	2-5%		
TOTAL	100%	XXXX	

Income/take-home pay = **XXXX**

Getting started: first things first. This may sound obvious, but as we begin we need to know what we're working with; our take-home pay (income after taxes and other fees) should be the number at the top of our budget. From there, every plan should start with "firstfruits" giving: tithe and offerings. God commands we offer a tithe, which literally means one tenth (Leviticus 27:32). In Genesis 4 two brothers, Cain and Abel, bring offerings to God. Abel brings "the firstborn of his flock and of their fat portions" and pleases God because he gives the first part of what he has (Genesis 4:4 ESV). We tithe on our firstfruits because it builds our faith and trust. We acknowledge God is the provider, trusting him for what is next.

It's easy to get hung up on questions such as, Should I tithe on the gross or net? Does God really mean exactly one tenth? Rather than getting legalistic about the amount, we should see one tenth as the starting place and then have fun from there! We can choose to give to our local church and to other organizations, but we can also look for countless other ways to give—anywhere from sending resources in the wake of a tragic natural disaster to picking up the dinner tab. Not only does God command the tithe (usually understood as what we give to the local church), he also asks for offerings—sacrificial giving above and beyond tithes (Deuteronomy 12:6; Malachi 3:8-10). Both are equally important to God because generosity matters. So let's make our tithe our first priority, include other offerings in our plan and look for ways each day to give sacrificially.

Savings and paying off debt (5-10%). Some people think that they should save whatever is left after spending what they want and pay only the bare minimum on debts if they have any. But in reality we should set aside money for savings at the beginning of the month and work to pay off debt as quickly as possible. Also, if we begin saving early on, our opportunity for compound interest on our savings far exceeds those who start a decade later. Keep this in mind if your company offers a 401(k) or IRA plan. Consider working with a trusted financial planner to become better informed and to make the most of potential investment opportunities.

Saving money. When it comes to saving money, recent alumni often want to know *why* they should be saving money and *how* to actually do it. We need vision for our money and reliable practices.

Just after graduation, I confess that I had no vision for my finances. I fell into what may sound like a strange pitfall—I got caught up in giving money to any charity or donation that came my way. Raised to give generously, I began giving away more than I was making. Before you think this sounds pious, I assure you it wasn't. I'm embarrassed by these early decisions with my dollars. I lacked financial planning, and though you could argue that I was giving to noble causes, I was not honoring God with my money management or even my motivations.

When my fiancé (now husband), Craig, confronted me, he observed, "I think you believe you are going to get a bigger crown in heaven for all your giving." Wow. As I reflected on his statement, the Spirit revealed my sin of trying to earn righteousness by my giving. Though Craig would confess that he suffered from a different money trap (buying a car he really couldn't afford right after college), we have both learned a ton about giving, spending and saving. We have also learned that the decisions you make in the first year or two out of college take some time to undo. We both wish we would have made better choices and taken the long view from the start.

So why should we save money? Because the Bible looks on it favorably (Proverbs 13:22) and because life is full of obstacles and opportunities. If we have money in the bank when life throws us a curve ball (our car breaks down, we incur medical expenses or we get laid off), we are less likely to totally strike out (become overwhelmed, get off track financially or go into unnecessary debt). One recent alum had a cycling accident during a brief lapse in medical insurance coverage. The cost of an ambulance ride and other bills amounted to thousands of dollars. She contacted me shortly after the incident, saying, "I'm so glad I was taught to have a hefty emergency fund. My life would have been so much worse without that."

Saving allows us to prepare for emergencies as well as for future opportunities such as pursing further education, traveling, starting a business or other venture, putting a down payment on a house, adopting a child or realizing whatever our dreams may hold. Also, saving positions us for the opportunity to give money away. There are endless needs around us. When we live within or below our means, we demonstrate our faithful stewardship of God's provision. We also experience the joy that comes when God provides opportunities for us to bless others, meet needs and pursue justice.

How do we save? In the very basic sense, we save money when we don't spend. We may be tempted to think we need a high-paying job in order to save. I know an alum who actually saved significantly more money after taking a pay cut of nearly *one-half* his salary! With the higher grossing job came the costs of eating out, expensive clothes and dry cleaning. The pay cut afforded him a lifestyle that cost much less— not to mention a quality of life that you cannot put a price tag on. So be mindful that the "good job" may not lead to the good life or lend to saving money.

Though I'd argue that the basics of saving money involve holding on to it, we must be mindful of the difference between saving and hoarding. The nuance is in our motivation and heart attitude. If we approach saving money with a scarcity mentality (if I don't grab it all now, it's going to go away and I'm not going to be okay), then we are hoarding (Proverbs 11:24-26). If we are greedy or stingy, we are on our way to ruin (Proverbs 28:22, 25). When it comes to our savings account, we acknowledge that God can give or take away at any moment. Our savings are not our security. Our security is in Christ alone, and our savings are simply an opportunity to honor him.

Lastly, there is a form of faulty thinking called prosperity theology that implies financial blessings are the will of God. Often this message comes in the form of "If you give to Christian ministries or churches, God will bless you with material blessings, health and wealth." Wealth is not a promise of the Christian life, and if God does entrust us with wealth, we are that much more responsible to steward it wisely.

As you're starting out you may feel like you're struggling to make ends meet, but if we land a higher paying job or begin to build wealth, we need to ask God how he wants us to use it. I was in a meeting with an accomplished individual who privately confessed that though she makes more than $100,000 a year, she lives on just over a third of it. The rest she invests in needs both locally and all over the world. We don't have to make six figures to give away money, but if we're blessed with a high salary, we should consider how we can give generously to fuel missions, ministry and other creative endeavors that spread the gospel and improve our world. It is the incredible generosity of individuals, especially our alumni, that funds me and my team in our work on campus. If a college ministry influenced your life, please consider investing in the future of that ministry by giving back!

Dealing with debt. So many homes, lives and institutions run on debt, and we have bought the lie that we need to go into debt to live a full life. We don't *need* to go into debt. We usually do because we want to or because we have not managed our risk. Generally people incur debt for schooling, houses, cars, vacations and other expenses or wants.

With the exception of going into debt for a home or property, the Bible does not look favorably on debt. Proverbs says, "The rich rule over the poor, and the borrower is slave to the lender" (22:7). In the New Testament Paul says, "Let no debt remain outstanding, except the continuing debt to love one another" (Romans 13:8). Debt is a noose that entangles us to the one we owe. And yet it is so easy to get caught up in it. If you do not have college loans or other debt, give thanks. If you do, make an aggressive plan to pay them off, consider alternatives before going into debt for higher education and avoid consumer debt.

In 2015, the average graduate with student loan debt owed $35,000. Even adjusted for inflation, that's more than twice what borrowers had to repay two decades earlier.[7]

When we commit to debt-free living—whether that's paying off school loans or credit cards or simply staying solvent so we don't incur more debt—there's an incredible peace and freedom that comes from it. Debt may tie us to a job or location we no longer like or limit us in other ways. But when we live debt free, we can make lifestyle changes. We benefit by not paying interest on our purchases, but also by having options. Also, we won't have the anxiety of choosing between paying the credit card bill and buying groceries.

Chelsea, a recent graduate who currently works for a nonprofit organization, has made a personal goal to become debt free by the time she turns twenty-five. Sticking to her budget plan each month, being prayerful about her finances and working a part-time waitressing job are three components of Chelsea's plan to reach her goal of paying off $30,000. On a minimal-moderate income, Chelsea sets aside money each month for giving, saving and paying off debt, and she does this without denying herself certain pleasures like the mini vacation she took to visit a friend (something she paid for by simply saving $50 per month in her travel budget). You can choose to pay off debt, give money away and save on nearly any income.

Deal with current debt and don't go into more. Avoid the pitfall of "zero percent financing, no money down" or the carefree swipe of the credit card. Practice self-denial and resist the temptation of instant gratification. Not only will your future self (or future spouse) thank you, but I trust that you will also experience the joy that comes from honoring God by your sacrifice and stewardship.

Housing, utilities and home repairs (25-38%). Though the cost of living ranges across the country and world, there are still general ways to save monthly on housing and utility costs. First, we need to keep our expectations in check. Many recent alumni think they will be able to live in the kinds of neighborhoods and homes that their own parents live in, when it's probably taken their parents the better part of a lifetime to afford their current house. Second, you should consider having roommates or housemates for a time, especially if you are living in a costly urban center. I know an alum who shared a three-bedroom *floor* of a house in Capitol Hill with four other roommates so they could live close to their jobs, split rent and utilities five ways and save thousands. When it comes to your home, furnishings and utilities, there are many things our society will convince us we need—our own space, cable TV, the fanciest phone or finest data plan. None of these things is inherently wrong, but sometimes we make sacrifices in certain areas that allow us more freedom and flexibility in other areas.

Automobile/transportation (12-15%). One pitfall many alumni fall into is the idea that they need a new car upon graduation, and that it's normal to have a car payment. The result: they may have a sweet ride, but they are saddled with a large payment on a depreciating asset. If your car payment is more than 15 percent of your income, you should probably be living in it! Seriously, strongly consider your car decision before going into debt. Why do I want this car? Is there another option that might work just as well? By saying yes to this car, what am I saying no to? Instead of making a car payment to a dealership, consider paying yourself (your savings account) each month until you save enough to pay cash for that next car (if you saved $400 per month for three years or so, you'd have $15,000 to spend).[8] Speaking from experience, this can be done!

Household (groceries, household items, gifts, clothes, haircuts, cosmetics) (15-25%). Some recent alumni are unprepared for the simple costs of keeping a fridge full and maintaining an apartment, while others are shocked by how quickly their dollars dwindle when they hit up happy hour or eat out multiple times a week (or day). How will you budget for the cost of basic food items? Will you clip coupons? Shop for sales? Eat mostly items in season? Prepare more of your own food instead of eating out? Another line item that seems to sink some alumni is gifts. Do you enjoy giving gifts (at weddings, birthdays, Christmas)? If so, how will you budget in advance so you can bless others with your generosity on these special occasions?

Entertainment and going out (including hobbies, gym membership) (5-10%). In a culture that encourages us to reward ourselves at every turn, this category may be one of the more challenging to keep in check. Whether it's Starbucks lattes or laziness when it comes to making dinner, it's easy to overspend on items for our enjoyment. At the same time, it's important to have something allotted here, especially if you are trying to establish yourself in a new community. Many social events revolve around food, and it's good to have a budget for this if possible. Whether it's bringing a dish to a potluck, taking someone out on a date or eating out after church with potential new friends, we should plan for fun. We are called to times of sacrifice and times of celebration. How can you cut back at certain times so you can celebrate at other times?

Insurance (5%). You'll want to budget a portion of your income for insurance coverage. Choosing insurance is about managing your risk; there's an initial cost that will likely save you from exorbitant future costs if you incur them (for example, renter's insurance may cost $10 per month, but if your apartment catches on fire you may save thousands when your insurance company fronts the bill for your lost items). When it comes to specific policies, plans and all of the different types of insurance, I urge you to do your homework. Ask good questions, acquire accurate information and make informed decisions. Though you may opt to forgo life insurance until you're married or drop collision insurance on your beater car, the main takeaway is to do what you can to manage your risk.

Miscellaneous (2-5%). Inevitably there are budget items unique to certain individuals as well as items that come up that we haven't planned for. You may consider allotting a small amount of money each month that you can use however you decide. Rather than dipping into other categories, you have margin to spend on unplanned items.

Ultimately you will have to decide the breakdown of your personal spending plan. Though your items and amounts may differ from your friends', every budget should result in a zero balance; the number you start with (income) should be spread across each category as you assign every dollar to a specific budget category. If you come in under budget, it's time to tell that extra amount where it will go.

FROM PAPER TO PRACTICE: PUT IT INTO ACTION

Our well-organized giving plan, commitment to save and desire to live debt free is only useful if we put it into action. Here are some pointers for taking those steps from paper to practice.

Find a system that works for you. You don't need to be an accounting major to keep accurate records of your finances, but it's important to find a budget-tracking system that works for you. For example, Chelsea credits her budget success to her use of the cash envelope system. Cash may feel archaic if we're used to plastic, but the tried and true envelope system works, especially for areas where overspending can happen more easily (such as entertainment and eating out). For each line item Chelsea keeps a cash envelope, fills it with the allotted amount at the start of the month, and when the money is gone she stops spending. Cash hurts a bit more to part with; statistically we spend more with a credit or debit card (about 12 to 18 percent more).[9] If you don't want to carry cash, you may opt to use an Excel spreadsheet, a virtual wallet (offered by a number of banks) or an online resource (like mint.com or youneedabudget.com).

Make it a discipline. Not only do we need a system, but we also need to stick to it. It means sitting down each month (or even once a week, at first) to track incoming and outgoing expenses. It can take about three months to see whether a budget actually works in real life (Did we budget enough for gasoline? Are we spending our allotted amount on groceries?). The only way to find out whether it works is to track it, and that takes discipline. As you start out, have grace with yourself for the months you blow the budget, and know there's a fresh start coming.

Find accountability. Though our culture has made money a taboo topic, it's important to have one trusted individual with whom we can share all of our financial information. If we're married, we should become one in the area of finances, budgeting together and holding each other accountable. If we're single, we should find a friend or mentor with whom we can check in about the state of our spending. Select someone who will encourage you, believe in you and tell you what you need to hear—not what you want to hear.

Start somewhere and celebrate success! Money can be overwhelming, so it's important to start somewhere. Make a budget (even if you don't have an income right now, practice with a starting salary number you can work with). Financial expert Dave Ramsey recommends we deal with necessities (food, utilities, housing, transportation) and then save and pay off debt from there.[10] If you are able to make a budget and use it, celebrate this huge accomplishment. From there, you can begin to work on these steps:

- Get $1,000 in the bank as an emergency fund. Or start with $500.

- Pay off debt. This will take time, but the sooner we are able to start, the better.

- Save three to six months' worth of expenses.

Each step of faithfulness will keep us moving along over time. Before we know it, we will look back in awe at how far we've come! When we stumble or fall, it's important to get back up. Failing in finances (or any part of life) happens when we refuse to get back up and try again.

Ultimately, my prayer is that you get into a right relationship with money. For you this may mean letting go of beliefs or actions that do not glorify God and adopting ones that do. God is honored when we manage money; our financial faithfulness is an act of worship. Because it's all God's, after all. We're just stewards. Though the enemy will try to trip us up, here's the hope and truth: through Christ all of our misuses of money can be redeemed. May we choose to trust and serve him, not money.

GOING DEEPER

1. How has our culture and your family of origin shaped your view of money?

2. How are you using money to worship God? Or are you worshiping money?

3. What money myths are you most likely to believe? Why? How can you walk in God's truth instead?

4. When it comes to the basics of a budget plan, what are some of your hopes or concerns?

5. What do you need to start, stop or continue doing so you can move from theory to practice?

6. What's one commitment you can make this week in living out a right relationship to money?

Scripture study: Proverbs 11:24-26; 28:22, 25; Ecclesiastes 5:10; Malachi 3:8-10; Matthew 6; 2 Corinthians 9:7; 1 Timothy 6:10

Recommended reading:

Randy Alcorn, *Managing God's Money: A Biblical Guide* (Carol Stream, IL: Tyndale House, 2011).

Mark Powley, *Consumer Detox: Less Stuff, More Life* (Grand Rapids: Zondervan, 2010).

Dave Ramsey, *Financial Peace Revisited* (New York: Viking Penguin, 2003).

"THE LAND IS GOOD"

TRUSTING A CONSTANT GOD
FOR DYNAMIC TIMES

And I will not pretend to know of all your pain
Just when you cannot then I will hold out faith for you
It's going to be alright.

SARA GROVES,
"IT'S GOING TO BE ALRIGHT"

THERE'S THAT POINT IN YOUR SENIOR YEAR or as a recent graduate when you start comparing yourself to others, especially if things aren't going well. One friend received a great job offer and you still don't have one. Someone else got in to graduate school, and another friend got engaged. Someone just posted a picture of their amazing life on social media. The comparison game begins, and it's easy to feel like we don't match up or that God is holding out on us.

Or maybe we feel completely overwhelmed. In one week we've experienced some of the lowest lows and highest highs, and we're not sure how to make sense of it all.

Or we feel like our lives are falling apart, and we're not sure where to turn.

In our deepest struggle, darkest hour and transitional times, we need to know it's going to be okay. We need hope.

IT'S GONNA BE OK (IGBOK)

In 2008, during a time when many people faced some of their darkest days, artist David Arms and his friend Lloyd Shadrack sat at a coffee shop and talked about hope. They said, "It was a time of unrest in the world and hope for many seemed to be teetering on the edge." Together they coined the term "igbok," defining it as "the universal language of hope." Since that day they've been spreading this message to many.[1]

Life is full of pain, fear, anxiety and loss. We have our hearts broken, we get rejected from the job we want, a parent receives a terminal diagnosis, we cannot please our employer no matter how hard we try, we fight with our roommate or spouse, our grandparent dies. Life is not as it ought to be, and we long for things to be okay. We need to know that our story is not over and that a promise of hope exists.

The founders of igbok believe it does. They believe that the God of the universe "shouted and whispered 'igbok' from Genesis to Revelation," making a promise and keeping it. God keeping his promise doesn't mean that the pain will go away but that we have a Savior, Christ, who has stepped down from heaven into our reality to restore this broken world and us. Because of this, "we can live this life with real hope—a hope that knows one day everything will be set right forever in the life to come."[2] It's gonna be okay. It really is.

As we forge our way after college, we hold deep hope for what God has in store. No matter what we are going through, we can say, "It's going to be okay." There's hope for tomorrow and hope for today. Hope is a strange thing because it both grounds us and lifts us. It is an anchor for the soul (Hebrews 6:19) and a helium balloon for the heart. Our hope is not in a job or a romantic relationship, in personal affluence or peace, but in the fact that the God of the universe sustains and carries us. So let's choose hope, no matter what. Because hope always leads.

WHAT IS THE *GOOD* LIFE?

As we talk about God having good in store for us, it's important to clarify what the good life really means. How our culture or we define it may not be the same as how God describes it. What is our definition? Making money? Enjoying entertainment, eating well, buying new things, taking vacations? I enjoy all of those, but that's not what it means to live. Life—true life—comes from Christ alone. No amount of money can buy the abundant life Jesus offers. And no lack can keep us from it. Life, bread, *all* we need comes from him. When we find true contentment in Christ, moment by moment, then we are *living*. It may not mean we are materially wealthy or physically healthy. It may not mean we feel comfortable or safe. Because, as my pastor puts it, "the good we want is not always the good we need."

God is interested in transforming our hearts so we can be more fully alive, and if we truly believe he can do this, there is no wilder ride than following Jesus. Author Annie Dillard says that if we fully comprehend the power of God, we should wear crash helmets in church and pass out life preservers and signal flares because we have no idea what he might do or where his power may take us.[3] This is living! The life Christ invites us into will likely not be easy, safe or convenient. But it will be *good*. It will be *best*. He has so much treasure in store if only we'd let go, open our palms and respond to his glorious invitation.

THE LAND IS GOOD

Not only does God promise good life, but he also promises that the "land" he's leading you to is good, wherever you're headed after college. In the same way God assured Abraham, Moses and all of his people that he had good life and good land in store, this promise stands today:

> For the LORD your God is bringing you into *a good land*, a land
> of brooks of water, of fountains and springs, flowing out in the
> valleys and hills, a land of wheat and barley, of vines and fig trees

and pomegranates, a land of olive trees and honey, a land in which you will eat bread without scarcity, *in which you will lack nothing*. (Deuteronomy 8:7-9 ESV, emphasis mine)

In transitional times it's easy to focus on our losses and lacks—those things we no longer have or that we wish to possess. Instead, let's trust that God is bringing us to a good place, filled with provision. This doesn't mean we'll avoid all hardship or that everything will be peachy when we arrive. But it does mean it will be good—everything we need.

BLESSED TO BE A BLESSING

God is choosing you, calling you and chasing after you. His character can be trusted. He is *God*. And, if you've said yes to him, you are *his*. As chapter one opened with God's call to Abraham to leave Harran, let's close by circling back to one of the most significant realities of Abraham's life: God's promise to him and for us that *we are blessed to be a blessing*.

God's blessing may not match our definition of blessing, but if we choose to follow him, we trust his hand is on us and his lavish grace soaks us. Living as people of this promise means that we seek to steward the grace God has given to us (Ephesians 3:2). We realize that it's not for us alone but for a greater purpose: to give away to others! Hour by hour, day by day we seek to share it—to find ways to bless every person and situation we find ourselves connected to. Instead of hoarding hope, we pass it along. Instead of living for ourselves, we seek to be living proof of a loving God.[4]

We are blessed to be a blessing in every circumstance, no matter how short the stint. In the transient time after college you may find yourself living with your parents for a few months, then moving for a temporary job or internship, then moving again. Resist the voices that say, "You're just passing through." We are called to plant (get connected) and bloom (thrive) wherever we are, for however long we are there.

In what has become a popular verse to pluck from Jeremiah, God says, "For I know the plans I have for you, . . . plans to prosper you and not to harm you, plans to give you hope and a future" (29:11). Maybe you have even received (or will receive) a graduation gift or card with those words. The truth of what God declares here should give us great hope, but let's not neglect to read those words in their larger context.

God led his people to the Promised Land, but there were also times in their history when the Israelites lived in places that felt far from a land of promise and hope. In Jeremiah 29, God speaks to his people who are exiled in the city of Babylon—an unfamiliar, even hostile place. He wants them to know that he has not forsaken them, even though living in Babylon is hard. Also he wants them to settle down in the city, plant gardens and grow their families. He wants them to plant and not pass through. Perhaps most importantly, he calls them to seek the peace and prosperity of the city to which he has called them. To pray for it and bless it. Because if it prospers, his people too will prosper (29:5-7).

God's hope for his people held captive in Babylon in the seventh century BC is no different for us today. If you've moved far from home or you're struggling at work, there may be days when you feel like you're in exile—lonely, uncomfortable or even oppressed. But the story doesn't end here. God has plans to prosper you, to pour out his provision. As we begin to root ourselves and invest in our community, we begin to experience the life of flourishing God intends. We *live into* the hope and future God has for us.

No matter where God calls and carries you after graduation, my prayer is that you choose to connect, commit and serve as a channel of grace. May you claim an unchanging promise in this dynamic time: *You are blessed to be a blessing.*

As you go, be filled and encouraged by this benediction (adapted from Numbers 6:24-26):

> The Lord bless you
> and keep you after college;
> the Lord make his face shine on you because you are his
> and be gracious to you because he is God;
> the Lord turn his face toward you (as you look to him)
> and give you deep peace that you can stand on him, a solid
> rock in every dynamic time.

ACKNOWLEDGMENTS

No work is ever our own. Our lives are a patchwork of the people and voices we encounter, and our work a tapestry of those influences—far too many to properly acknowledge in these short pages. That said, I want to do my best to credit those who have made this book possible. With deep gratitude, I want to say thank you:

To the Senior EXIT team past and present. Our ministry would not exist if not for the passion, ideas and people behind it: Johnny Pons, Hannah Ingram, Cheryl and Bill Bonner, Lara Echerd, Janae DelMaestro, Steve Logue, Jenna Greaser, Sarah Cowart, John Henderson, Jonathan Helter, Cameisha Williams, Jess Kappes, Scott Welliver and the many guest speakers and panelists who serve us.

To the Calvary staff team, especially those who have coached or mentored me or whom I have served alongside on the Elements team: Dan and Lynn Nold, Dan and Christina Dorsey, Sherilyn Jameson, Vic King, Stacy Sublett, Steve Lutz, Caleb Rebarchak, Mike Swanson, Nick Hiner, Mikala Hursh, Kristen Lawton, Leann Keller, Andrea Redhair, Josh Felstead and Dana Ray. You challenge me to dream big, remind me of God's grace and make me laugh.

To my ministry partners at Penn State. Senior EXIT would not thrive if not for the support of leaders past and present within ACF, Burning Hearts, Cru, CSF, DCF, ICF, InterVarsity, Navs, New Life and VCF. I'm blessed to colabor with you.

To my CCO colleagues and associates, especially those who have led and mentored me and called out my gifts. Your influence and support has significantly shaped me and my ministry: Dan Dupee,

Vince Burens, Nicole Shirk, Charity Haubrich, Dave McBride, Scott Evans, Phil Shiavoni, Derek Melleby, Byron Borger, Sam Van Eman, Scott Calgaro, Keith Martel and Linda Leon.

To my professors at Messiah College and Geneva College, especially those who have invested in me far beyond my time in the classroom: Crystal Downing, Jonathan Lauer, Christopher Couch, Julia Kasdorf, Helen Walker, Don Opitz, Terry Thomas and Paul Blezien. You have ignited my love for learning and pushed me toward my best work.

To Chris Willard and Leadership Network, and to Brian Frye and Collegiate Collective. You have facilitated collaboration that makes the whole of our ministries far greater than the sum of their parts.

To those who read the earliest drafts of the manuscript, later drafts or select chapters: Julia Davis, Sarah Bednarcik, Kate Bowman-Johnston, Megan Colabrese, Kimi Cunningham Grant, Beth Anderson, Faye Poon, Dana Ray, Jonathan Hagood and the senior seminar students at Hope College. Your feedback improved this book immensely.

To my editor, Al Hsu, and the team at IVP. You have not only shepherded this project with wisdom and excellence, but you have also cared for me so well in the process.

To the students and alumni who generously allowed me to tell their stories. You inspire me and remind me of the importance of our work.

To the members of my community in State College and beyond who are not already mentioned here. You are a constant reminder of God's abundant provision.

Last, I want to thank those who believed in this before it was a "this." I owe Steve Lutz and Derek Melleby not only for telling me I could do it, but also for coaching me throughout the process. I'm forever indebted to Kate Filer and Lisa Rieck for the sacrifices they've made: reading and rereading drafts, rooting for me over the *years* and praying for me continually. My family has also been a constant source of love and support, especially my parents, Marie and Roger Young and Gail and Vern Reitz, and my siblings, Julia and Kyle Davis and Megan and Kenny Platt. Finally, *thank you* will always feel too tiny a phrase to contain all I want to say to my husband, Craig. I'm so grateful for the ways you push me to my potential and believe in me every step of the way. You and our children are God's richest gifts to me: living proof that he loves to lavish us in life after college.

APPENDIX A

IDENTITY IN CHRIST

THERE ARE A THOUSAND WORDS we can use to *describe* ourselves after college, but these descriptors do not *define* us. Our identity—who we are—is defined by God alone, not by our shifting friendships, job performance or relationship status. In a transitional time it's normal to doubt ourselves or question our place in the world, but at the end of the day (and the beginning) we can choose to let one thing define us: Jesus Christ.

Who am I?

- I am the salt of the earth (Matt. 5:13).

- I am the light of the world (Matt. 5:14).

- I am a child of God (John 1:12).

- I am a part of the true vine, a channel of Christ's life (John 15:1, 5).

- I am Christ's friend (John 15:15).

- I am chosen and appointed by Christ to bear His fruit (John 15:16).

- I am a slave of righteousness (Rom. 6:18).

- I am enslaved to God (Rom. 6:22).

- I am a joint heir with Christ, sharing His inheritance with Him (Rom. 8:17).

- I am a temple—a dwelling place—of God. His Spirit and His life dwell in me (1 Cor. 3:16; 6:19).

- I am united to the Lord and am one in spirit with Him (1 Cor. 6:17).

- I am a member of Christ's Body (1 Cor. 12:27; Eph. 5:30).

- I am a new creation (2 Cor. 5:17).

- I am reconciled to God and am a minister of reconciliation (2 Cor. 5:18, 19).
- I am a saint (1 Cor. 1:2; Eph. 1:1; Phil. 1:1; Col. 1:2).
- I am God's workmanship—His handiwork—born anew in Christ to do His work (Eph. 2:10).
- I am a fellow citizen with the rest of God's family (Eph. 2:19).
- I am a prisoner of Christ (Eph. 3:1; 4:1).
- I am righteous and holy (Eph. 4:24).
- I am a citizen of heaven, seated in heaven right now (Eph. 2:6; Phil. 3:20).
- I am hidden with Christ in God (Col. 3:3).
- I am an expression of the life of Christ because He is my life (Col. 3:4).
- I am chosen of God, holy and dearly loved (Col. 3:12; 1 Thess. 1:4).
- I am a holy partaker of Christ; I share in His life (Heb. 3:14).
- I am one of God's living stones, being built up in Christ as a spiritual house (1 Pet. 2:5).
- I am a member of a chosen race, a royal priesthood, a holy nation, a people for God's own possession (1 Pet. 2:9, 10).
- I am an alien and stranger to this world in which I temporarily live (1 Pet. 2:11).
- I am an enemy of the devil (1 Pet. 5:8).
- I am a child of God and I will resemble Christ when He returns (1 John 3:1, 2).
- I am born of God, and the evil one—the devil—cannot touch me (1 John 5:18).

This list is taken from Neil T. Anderson, Victory Over the Darkness *(Ventura, CA: Regal Books, 1990), 51-53. Used by permission of Bethany House Publishers, a division of Baker Publishing Group.*

MONTHLY BUDGET PLAN

Budget Item	Percentage Budgeted	Amount Budgeted	Amount Spent
Tithe/offerings (10-15%): includes tithe to a local church, as well as charities and other offerings			
Savings (10-15%): includes an emergency fund (three to six months of living expenses), a retirement fund (could be through an employer's 401(k)) and big purchases (car, first home, etc.)			
Debt repayment (5-10%): includes college loans, as well as consumer/credit debt and car payments (Note: the goal is to pay down the principle of your debt as soon as possible to save on interest.)			
Housing (25-35%): includes mortgage or rent, property taxes, repairs/maintenance and association dues			
Utilities (5-10%): includes electricity, gas, water, trash, phone, Internet and cable			
Food (5-15%): includes groceries and restaurants			

The purpose of a budget is to make a plan for our income so we can live within (or below) our means, save for the future and give generously. When we assign every dollar a home, we tell our money where to go rather than the other way around. While each person and family will tailor their budget to their unique needs and priorities, this chart provides some basic categories and suggested allocations.

For additional budget resources, try Dave Ramsey, You Need a Budget and Mint. All have online templates that can get you budgeting in minutes!

PERSONALITY AND STRENGTHS ASSESSMENTS

HERE ARE A FEW ASSESSMENTS that can help you understand your strengths, personality and purpose. Keep in mind, often the best discovery happens with others and when we're actually doing stuff!

GALLUP'S CLIFTON STRENGTHSFINDER ASSESSMENT

"Gallup research proves that people succeed when they focus on what they do best."[1] Gallup offers the StrengthsFinder Assessment, which identifies thirty-four talent themes to help people discover their potential strengths. "When they identify their talents and develop them into strengths, people are more productive, perform better, and are more engaged."[2]

The entry-level assessment reveals our top five talent themes (our "unique combination of skills, talents, and knowledge—also known as strengths") and gives us a way to discuss and develop them.[3] Understanding our strengths can help us discern the type of work that allows us to do what we do best.
www.gallupstrengthscenter.com

DISC PERSONALITY ASSESSMENT

Understanding our personality style and others' promotes effective teamwork and healthy interpersonal communication. The DISC assessment, which identifies four behavioral styles, reveals our dominant personality and helps to guide us as we connect with others. When we understand our behavioral tendencies, we can not only improve communication, but also learn why certain activities or interactions give us energy and others drain us.

There are numerous websites that offer DISC personality tests; I use Personality Insights. Select from a number of different Discovery Reports that will reveal your style. www.personality-insights.com

SHAPE INVENTORY

In *The Purpose Driven Life*, Rick Warren uses the acronym SHAPE to help us identify how we've been uniquely shaped by God. SHAPE stands for

S: Spiritual Gifts—special abilities that God has given us to share his love and serve others.

H: Heart, which refers to our God-given passions and interests.

A: Abilities, which can often include nonspiritual, natural gifts.

P: Personality—the unique ways we think and relate to the world around us.

E: Experiences, both positive and negative, that provide us a context from which to empathize with and minister to others.[4]

Rick Warren, *The Purpose Driven Life Study Guide*, vol. 5, *You Were Shaped for Serving God*, www.saddlebackresources.com/products/the -purpose-driven-life-shaped-for-serving-god-vol-5-study-guide (covers chapters 29 to 35 from *The Purpose Driven Life*)

NOTES

CHAPTER 1: "GO TO AN UNKNOWN LAND"

[1]Although Genesis records the details of God changing Abram's name to Abraham in a later chapter as connected to the covenant of circumcision he makes with Abram (Genesis 17:5), for the purposes of continuity all references in this book to Abram/Abraham will appear as Abraham.

[2]John H. Walton, *The NIV Application Commentary: Genesis* (Grand Rapids: Zondervan, 2001), 399.

[3]Ibid.

[4]Ibid.

[5]Ibid.

[6]See Jeffery Arnett, *Emerging Adulthood: The Winding Road from the Late Teens Through the Twenties* (New York: Oxford University Press, 2004).

[7]Philip Graham Ryken, *Christian Worldview: A Student's Guide* (Wheaton, IL: Crossway, 2013), 20.

[8]See Steven Garber, *The Fabric of Faithfulness: Weaving Together Belief and Behavior*, expanded ed. (Downers Grove, IL: InterVarsity Press, 2007).

[9]See Jeffery Arnett, *Emerging Adulthood: The Winding Road from the Late Teens Through the Twenties* (New York: Oxford University Press, 2004), chaps. 1 and 10.

[10]Jim Wallis, "Building Global Justice: We Are the Ones We Have Been Waiting For" (Stanford baccalaureate address, June 12, 2004).

[11]See Beth Moore, *Believing God* (Nashville: B&H, 2004) and the related Bible study curriculum.

[12]Anne Lamott, *Bird by Bird* (New York: Anchor Books, 1994), 18.

[13]Ann Voskamp, "When You're Feeling a Bit Broken," *A Holy Experience* (blog), April 4, 2011, www.aholyexperience.com/2011/04/when-youre-feeling-a-bit-broken-free-weekly-gratitude-journal.

CHAPTER 2: IN TRANSITION

[1]William Bridges, *Transitions: Making Sense of Life's Changes* (Cambridge, MA: Da Capo, 2004), xii-xiv, 18, 129-30.

[2]This is a phrase my pastor, Dan Nold, uses when he talks with our seniors.

[3]Terry Walling, *Stuck! Navigating the Transitions of Life and Leadership* (Chico, CA: Leader Breakthru, 2008), 27.

[4]Bridges, *Transitions*, 3.

[5]Ibid.

[6]Ibid., 113-15.

[7]Ibid., 134.

[8]Ibid., 145, 171.

[9]Sherry Turkle, "Stop Googling. Let's Talk," *The New York Times*, September 27, 2015, www.nytimes.com/2015/09/27/opinion/sunday/stop-googling -lets-talk.html?_r=0.

[10]Ibid.

[11]Bridges, *Transitions*, 158.

[12]Mary Oliver, *Blue Iris: Poems and Essays* (Boston: Beacon Press, 2004), 17.

[13]Bridges, *Transitions*, 160.

[14]Ibid., 159.

CHAPTER 3: TAKE UP YOUR CROSS

[1]Lisa Graham McMinn, *The Contented Soul* (Downers Grove, IL: Inter-Varsity Press, 2006), 45.

[2]Compiled by Erin James, "Q & A with Your New *Daily Collegian* Columnists," *Daily Collegian*, September 15, 2004. Their answers: our sense of entitlement, apathy, inflexibility, we don't like to look at other sides of issues or change our ways, too spoiled, lack of respect, social apathy and a feeling of entitlement.

[3]"Fortitude," Merriam-Webster, www.merriam-webster.com/dictionary /fortitude.

[4]Ann Voskamp, *One Thousand Gifts* (Grand Rapids: Zondervan, 2010).

[5]A. W. Tozer, *The Pursuit of God* (Minneapolis: Bethany House, 2013), 82.

[6]Ibid., 87.

[7]Wesley Hill, "Yes, Many Christian Communities Are Toxic for My LBGT Friends. But There's More," *The Washington Post*, July 15, 2015, www.wash ingtonpost.com/news/acts-of-faith/wp/2015/07/15/yes-many-christian-communities-are-toxic-for-my-lbgt-friends-but-theres-more.

[8]Ibid.

CHAPTER 4: THE TYRANNY OF CHOICE

[1]I am indebted to Cheryl Bonner for shaping my views on this topic as she shares with our seniors each year.

[2]James Petty, *Step by Step: Divine Guidance for Ordinary Christians* (Phillipsburg, NJ: P&R, 1999).

[3]Ibid., 59.

[4]Kevin DeYoung, *Just Do Something* (Chicago: Moody Publishers, 2009), 19.

[5]Ibid., 42-43.

[6]A. W. Tozer, *The Pursuit of God* (Minneapolis: Bethany House, 2013), 87-88. I'm also indebted to Sam Van Eman for influencing my perspective on this when he shared the concept with our seniors.

[7]Petty, *Step by Step*, 193-228. Petty lists these steps as the first four of his "Seven Elements of Biblical Decision Making." His last three elements are meditation, decision and expectation.

[8]Ibid., 197.

[9]Ibid., 200.

[10]DeYoung, *Just Do Something*, 36.

[11]Andy Stanley, *The Best Question Ever* (Colorado Springs: Multnomah Books, 2004), 28.

CHAPTER 5: BEYOND THE QUAD

[1]Melissa Tucker, "Making, Breaking, and Keeping Friendships," in *Results May Vary: Christian Women Reflect on Post-College Life*, edited by Linda Beail and Sylvia Cortez (San Diego: Point Loma, 2013), 28.

[2]I am indebted to Laurie Checkley, CCO staff seminar speaker, for shaping my view on this topic. Much of the content in this section and in "Practice Hospitality: Welcoming the Stranger" are directly inspired by a talk she gave and notes she shared: "Intentional Friendship," CCO Staff Seminar, Laurelville, PA, January 2008.

[3]William Shakespeare, *As You Like It*.

[4]Gregory L. Jones, "Discovering Hope Through Holy Friendships," Faith and Leadership, June 18, 2012, www.faithandleadership.com/l-gregory -jones-discovering-hope-through-holy-friendships.

[5]Adam S. McHugh, *Introverts in the Church: Finding Our Place in an Extrovert Culture* (Downers Grove, IL: InterVarsity Press, 2009), 101-6.

[6]Martin Hallett, "Friendship," True Freedom Trust, www.truefreedomtrust .co.uk/node/21.

[7]Meg Jay, *The Defining Decade: Why Your Twenties Matter—and How to Make the Most of Them Now* (New York: Twelve/Hachette Book Group, 2012), 44.

[8]Henri Nouwen, *Reaching Out: The Three Movements of the Spiritual Life* (New York: Image Books/Doubleday, 1975), 71.

[9]Ibid., 66-67.

[10]Ibid., 65.

[11]Johnny Pons brings this content to our EXIT students each year. I also found this article helpful in shaping this section: Paul R. Martin, "Be a Barnabas; Pursue a Paul; Train a Timothy," *Enrichment Journal*, http://enrichmentjournal.ag.org/200702/200702_000_barnabas.cfm.

CHAPTER 6: NO PERFECT CHURCH

[1]The discussion of the word *church* in this section has been influenced by a talk given by Pastor Dan Nold, staff retreat at Calvary Church, State College, PA, July 2013.

[2]See Soong-Chan Rah, *The Next Evangelicalism: Freeing the Church from Western Cultural Captivity* (Downers Grove, IL: InterVarsity Press, 2009), chaps. 7–9.

[3]See Josh White, "Vienna Presbyterian Church Seeks Forgiveness, Redemption in Wake of Abuse Scandal," *The Washington Post*, April 2, 2011, www.washing tonpost.com/local/vienna-presbyterian-church-works-to-overcome-revela tions-of-sexual-abuse/2011/03/30/AF3hNxQC_story.html.

CHAPTER 7: PEOPLE ARE STRANGE

[1]Tracy Chevalier, *Girl with a Pearl Earring* (New York: Plume, 1999), 26-27.

[2]Ibid., 27.

[3]Jessica Jackley, talk at Jubilee Conference, 2009, http://vimeo.com/8545171.

[4]Sherry Turkle, "Stop Googling. Let's Talk," *The New York Times*, September 26, 2015, www.nytimes.com/2015/09/27/opinion/sunday/stop-googling -lets-talk.html?_r=0.

[5]Harper Lee, *To Kill a Mockingbird*, 50th anniversary ed. (1960; repr., New York: HarperCollins, 2002), 33.

[6]Turkle, "Stop Googling. Let's Talk."

[7]Tomas Spath and Cassandra Dahnke, quoted in "What Is Civility?," The Institute for Civility in Government, 2016, www.instituteforcivility.org /who-we-are/what-is-civility.

[8]Jeff Flake and Martin Heinrich, "Two Opposing Senators, a Deserted Island and an Idea," *The Washington Post*, October 22, 2014, www.washing tonpost.com/opinions/two-opposing-senators-a-deserted-island-and-an -idea/2014/10/21/127ef9e6-579c-11e4-bd61-346aee66ba29_story.html.

[9]Philip Yancey, *Vanishing Grace* (Grand Rapids: Zondervan, 2014), 26.

CHAPTER 8: FAMILY MATTERS

[1]See Meg Jay, *The Defining Decade: Why Your Twenties Matter—and How to Make the Most of Them Now* (New York: Twelve/Hachette Book Group, 2012).

[2]I'm indebted to Johnny Pons and Gary and Joani Brown for their collaboration on the resource "Relating to Your Parents Post-College," which we share with seniors each year (available at www.seniorexit.com/wp-content /uploads/2013/01/EXIT_family_doc_onesheet.pdf). Some of the content from that resource appears in various parts of this chapter.

[3]Anne Lamott, *Traveling Mercies: Some Thoughts on Faith* (New York: Anchor Books, 1999), 219-20.

[4]Pastor Dan Nold shares this when he addresses our seniors on this topic.

[5]Richard Fry, "More Millennials Living with Family Despite Improved Job Market," Pew Research Center, July 29, 2015, www.pewsocialtrends.org /2015/07/29/more-millennials-living-with-family-despite-improved-job -market. In this study "young adults" includes ages eighteen to thirty-four.

CHAPTER 9: TWENTY-SOMETHING RELATIONSHIPS

[1]This topic is too important and complex to open up in this short chapter. As I've walked with students who struggle with same-sex attraction or knowing how to respond to friends who identify as LGBT, I've found these resources to be most helpful: Wesley Hill, *Washed and Waiting*; Sam Allberry, *Is God Anti-Gay?*; Chad W. Thompson, *Loving Homosexuals as Jesus Would*; Jenell Williams Paris, *The End of Sexual Identity*; and Andrew Marin, *Love Is an Orientation*.

[2]See Meg Jay, *The Defining Decade: Why Your Twenties Matter—and How to Make the Most of Them Now* (New York: Twelve/Hachette Book Group, 2012). The book's core concept is that our twenties matter. The thirties are not the new twenties. Though Jay doesn't take a faith approach or address sex, dating and marriage exclusively, she does tackle these topics, and her thesis is this: the decisions we make in this decade define us beyond it.

[3]See Timothy Keller, *The Meaning of Marriage: Facing the Complexities of Commitment with the Wisdom of God* (New York: Dutton, 2011), 33-37.

[4]David Kim, *20 and Something: Have the Time of Your Life (And Figure It All Out Too)* (Grand Rapids: Zondervan, 2013), 25.

[5]Karen Swallow Prior, "The Case for Getting Married Young," *The Atlantic*, March 22, 2013, www.theatlantic.com/sexes/archive/2013/03/the-case-for -getting-married-young/274293.

[6]Prior, "The Case for Getting Married Young"; Kim, *20 and Something*, 70.

[7]Prior, "The Case for Getting Married Young."

[8]Amie Gordon, "The 'Cohabitation Effect': The Consequences of Premarital Cohabitation," *Psych Your Mind* (blog), August 20, 2012, http://psych-your -mind.blogspot.com/2012/08/the-cohabitation-effect-consequences-of .html.

[9]Amie Gordon, "The 'Cohabitation Effect': The Consequences of Premarital Cohabitation."

[10]Lauren Winner, *Real Sex: The Naked Truth About Chastity* (Grand Rapids: Brazos, 2005), 50.

[11]Lisa Graham McMinn, *Sexuality and Holy Longing: Embracing Intimacy in a Broken World* (San Francisco: Jossey-Bass, 2004), 172.

[12]Winner, *Real Sex*, 38.

[13]Alex Williams, "The End of Courtship?," *The New York Times*, January 13, 2013, www.nytimes.com/2013/01/13/fashion/the-end-of-courtship.html ?pagewanted=all&_r=0.

[14]I'm indebted to Johnny Pons for introducing these levels to me and our seniors. These five levels come from Pastor Brad Sprague.

[15]Albert Y. Hsu, *Singles at the Crossroads: A Fresh Perspective on Christian Singleness* (Downers Grove, IL: InterVarsity Press, 1997), 74.

[16]Mindy Meier, *Sex and Dating: Questions You Wish You Had Answers To* (Downers Grove, IL: InterVarsity Press, 2007), 32.

CHAPTER 10: ON PURPOSE

I'm indebted to Don Opitz for shaping my views on this topic, especially his lecture "Vocation and Calling," June 23, 2004, in Introduction to Campus Worldviews (HED 504). My notes from that course appear in sections of this chapter. I'm also indebted to Steven Garber, Crystal Downing, Mary Elizabeth Anderson, Bethany Jenkins, Kimi Cunningham Grant and Julia Davis for the ways that conversations with them have further clarified my views on this topic.

[1]Steven Garber, *Visions of Vocation: Common Grace for the Common Good* (Downers Grove, IL: InterVarsity Press, 2014), 12.

[2]Karen Yates, "Your Calling Is Closer Than You Think," *Relevant*, May 28, 2013, www.relevantmagazine.com/god/practical-faith/your-calling-closer -you-think.

[3]Ibid.

[4]Quentin Schultze, *Here I Am: Now What on Earth Should I Be Doing?* (Grand Rapids: Baker Books, 2005), 9-10.

[5]Bethany Jenkins talked about "prototyping" at the Faith, Life, and Work Conference, Calvary Church, Harvest Fields, Boalsburg, PA, November 7, 2015.

[6]Schultze, *Here I Am*, 12.

[7]Gordon Smith, *Courage and Calling: Embracing Your God-Given Potential*, rev. ed. (Downers Grove, IL: InterVarsity Press, 2011), 84-85.

[8]Schultze, *Here I Am*, 17.

[9]Christina Vuleta, "Twenty-Somethings: What You Risk by Switching Jobs Too Often," *Huffington Post*, March 19, 2011, www.huffingtonpost.com /christina-vuleta/career-change_b_836473.html; see also Robin Marantz Henig, "What Is It About 20-Somethings?," *The New York Times*, August 18, 2010, www.nytimes.com/2010/08/22/magazine/22Adulthood-t.html? _r=1&pagewanted=all.

[10]Zora Neale Hurston, *Their Eyes Were Watching God* (Philadelphia: J. B. Lippincott, 1937), 21.

[11]Lee Hardy, *The Fabric of This World: Inquiries into Calling, Career Choice, and the Design of Human Work* (Grand Rapids: Eerdmans, 1990), 80.

[12]Ibid, 92.

[13]This paragraph is directly inspired by a phone conversation with Beth Anderson on October 27, 2015.

[14]Terri Frase Furton, "Terri's Story," in *Imagining Impossibilities: Stories of Westmont Alumni Women 1988–2003*, compiled, edited and printed by Shirley A. Mullen, April 2007. Used by permission.

[15]Emilie Wapnick, "Why Some of Us Don't Have One True Calling," TED, April 2015, www.ted.com/talks/emilie_wapnick_why_some_of_us_don_t _have_one_true_calling?language=en.

[16]Elizabeth Barrett Browning, "Aurora Leigh," in *The Oxford Book of English Mystical Verse*, ed. Daniel H. S. Nicholson and Arthur H. E. Lee (Oxford: Clarendon Press, 1917), www.bartleby.com/236/86.html.

[17]Garber, *Visions of Vocation*, 51.

[18]Ibid., 140

CHAPTER 11: A FAITH THAT WORKS

I'm indebted to Mark L. Russell, Derek Melleby and Sam Van Eman for shaping my views on this topic.

[1]Sam Crabtree, "Words of Wisdom," in *In Transition*, ed. Rick James (Orlando: Crupress, 2006), 147.

[2]Joyce Jarek, conversation with the author, March 31, 2015.

[3]Wendell Berry, "Christianity and the Survival of Creation," in *The Art of the Commonplace: The Agrarian Essays of Wendell Berry*, ed. Norman Wirzba (Berkeley, CA: Counterpoint, 2002), 315.

[4]Jamin Roller, "Work and Worldview," *The Village Blog*, November 10, 2015, www.thevillagechurch.net/the-village-blog/work-and-worldview.

[5]Mark Russell, *Our Souls at Work: How Great Leaders Live Their Faith in the Global Marketplace* (Boise, ID: Russell Media, 2010), 24.

[6]Gabe Lyons, *The Next Christians: How a New Generation Is Restoring the Faith* (New York: Doubleday, 2010), 115-16.

[7]Al Hsu, "The Dilbertization of Work," in "Vocation," ed. Robert B. Kruschwitz, *Christian Reflection* (Waco, TX: The Center for Christian Ethics at Baylor University, 2004), www.baylor.edu/ifl/christianreflection/Vocation articleHsu.pdf.

[8]See Amy Sherman, *Kingdom Calling: Vocational Stewardship for the Common Good* (Downers Grove, IL: InterVarsity Press, 2011).

[9]Mark L. Russell, "Our Souls at Work," Jubilee Conference workshop, Pittsburgh, PA, February 19, 2011.

[10]"Katherine Leary Alsdorf: We're Made to Work," interview, *Faith & Leadership*, January 29, 2013, www.faithandleadership.com/qa/katherine-leary -alsdorf-were-made-work?page=0%2C0.

[11]Daniel H. Pink, "Drive: The Summaries," Daniel H. Pink official website, last modified January 2016, www.danpink.com/drive-the-summaries.

CHAPTER 12: FINANCIAL FAITHFULNESS

I am indebted to Dave Seibel for shaping my views on this topic as he shares with our seniors every year. Dave and I have both been heavily influenced by financial expert Dave Ramsey. Much of this chapter's content comes from

Ramsey's Financial Peace University course as well as the companion book, Dave Ramsey, *Financial Peace Revisited* (New York: Viking Penguin, 2003).

[1]Answers to the true/false statements:

- According to the Bible, money is the root of all evil. *False.* See I Timothy 6:10: "For the *love* of money is the root of all kinds of evil." (emphasis mine)

- If you buy a $200,000 home (with a 20 percent down payment) at a 5 percent interest rate and pay it back over thirty years, you will actually pay over $300,000 to own that home. *True.* See www.mortgage calculator.org.

- A car payment is unavoidable for recent graduates. *False* (with a few exceptions). While some recent graduates may need to take out a small loan to purchase a car so they can get to and from work (in locations that don't offer public transportation), we usually go into debt for a vehicle (or a nicer vehicle) because we want to, not because we need to.

- The average consumer spends 12 to 18 percent more when paying with a credit card versus cash. *True.* Andrew Beattie, "Should You Pay in Cash?," Investopedia, accessed January 23, 2016, www.investopedia .com/articles/pf/08/pay-in-cash.asp.

- Ann saves $200 per month, starting at age 18 and stopping at age 28 ($24,000 saved). John saves $200 per month, starting at age 28 and stopping at age 65 ($88,000 saved). Both average 10 percent in annual interest until age 65. Because of *compound interest*, Ann has $1.4 million and John has $870,000. *True.* See www.thecalculatorsite.com /finance/calculators/compoundinterestcalculator.php.

[2]Dave Ramsey uses this verse to talk about how "money is amoral" (*Financial Peace Revisited*, 20).

[3]The New York Times, "Greece's Debt Crisis Explained," *The New York Times*, updated November 9, 2015, www.nytimes.com/interactive/2015 /business/international/greece-debt-crisis-euro.html?_r=0.

[4]Robert Harrow, "Average Credit Card Debt in America: 2016 Facts & Figures," ValuePenguin, accessed February 25, 2016, www.valuepenguin .com/average-credit-card-debt.

[5]John H. Pryor et al., *The American Freshman: National Norms Fall 2010* (Los Angeles: Higher Education Research Institute, UCLA, 2010), 8, 38; available at http://heri.ucla.edu/pr-display.php?prQry=55. Terry Thomas also discussed this change in educational motivation when he spoke at the

Faith, Life Conference, Calvary Church, Harvest Fields, Boalsburg, PA, November 7, 2015.

[6]The information in this section comes from Dave Siebel who also borrows from Dave Ramsey. See Ramsey, *Financial Peace Revisited*, 292-310.

[7]Jeffrey Sparshott, "Congratulations, Class of 2015. You're the Most Indebted Ever (For Now)," *Real Time Economics* (blog), *The Wall Street Journal*, May 8, 2015, http://blogs.wsj.com/economics/2015/05/08/congratulations-class -of-2015-youre-the-most-indebted-ever-for-now.

[8]Dave Ramsey talks about this concept in *Financial Peace Revisited*, 57-59, 116-17.

[9]Andrew Beattie, "Should You Pay in Cash?," *Investopedia*, accessed January 23, 2016, www.investopedia.com/articles/pf/08/pay-in-cash.asp.

[10]Ramsey, *Financial Peace Revisited*, 273-74.

CONCLUSION: "THE LAND IS GOOD"

[1]"What Is igbok?," It's Gonna Be O.K. website, accessed February 25, 2016, https://igbok.com/about.

[2]Ibid.

[3]Annie Dillard, *Teaching a Stone to Talk: Expectations and Encounters* (New York: HarperCollins, 2013), 44.

[4]I'm not sure where this originates, but my pastor, Dan Nold, challenges us to act in such a manner that we are living proof of a loving God.

APPENDIX C: PERSONALITY AND STRENGTHS ASSESSMENTS

[1]Gallup, "Boost Your Talents with Clifton StrengthsFinder®," Gallup Strengths Center, accessed January 24, 2016, www.gallupstrengthscenter .com/Purchase/en-US/Index.

[2]Ibid.

[3]Ibid.

[4]Brandon Cox, "How to Discover Your Spiritual Gifts," Pastors.com, June 28, 2011, http://pastors.com/how-to-discover-your-spiritual-gifts.

ABOUT THE AUTHOR

ERICA YOUNG REITZ directs Senior EXIT, a one-year experience that prepares graduating college seniors for the transition into the next phase of life. She works for the Coalition for Christian Outreach (CCO) in partnership with Calvary Church, reaching out to students at Penn State University. Erica has an MA in higher education from Geneva College, with a graduate research focus on the senior-year transition. She and her husband, Craig, live in State College, Pennsylvania, with their two children.

For more information or to contact the author, visit aftercollegetransition.com.

ABOUT THE CCO

The Coalition for Christian Outreach (ccojubilee.org) is a campus ministry organization that calls college students to serve Jesus with their entire lives.

Our ministry is distinct in three ways:

1. We develop students to be passionate leaders who serve Jesus Christ in their studies, jobs, communities and families.

2. We serve together with the church, inviting students into the lives of local congregations.

3. We design each ministry to fit the needs of every campus we serve.